GRANA

ITS HISTORY
OUR HERITAGE

Editors:
Joy Burns
Bernadette Grier

JUNE 1987

Reprinted April 1995
New and Revised Edition November 2002

Published by: Granard Guild, I.C.A.

Pages 127 to 184 sponsored by Longford Community Resources Limited under the LEADER II Programme.

ISBN: 0 9512101 2 2

Printed by: Turner Print Group, Longford.

LIST OF CONTENTS

Coat of Arms	3
Introduction	4
History of Granard	5
Town Commissioners	27
Street Names	29
Special Features	33
Churches	39
A Walk Around Granard	52
Schools	54
People of Granard	68
Traces of Irish in everyday use in the Granard Area	76
Rivers & Lakes	78
Flora & Fauna	81
Townlands	83
Local Placenames	85
Trades & Transport	86
Fairs & Markets	94
Sport	99
Folklore	106
Entertainment	119
The Harper's Land	123
Granard in the Eighties	125

2002 SECTION

The 2002 Excavation at Granardkill, Co. Longford	129
Maps of the Granard area	139
Useful map sources for Granard	142
The Motte — further reflections	145
Archaeological Sites around Granard	146
Details of Sites in the Granard area	147
Lake Settlements in Lough Kinale	148
The Flax and Linen Industry in Granard Barony	150
Glossary of terms used in the Flax and Linen Industry	152
Granard Union Workhouse	153
Famine folklore / St. Patrick's Church, Granard	158
1798 – Battle of Granard	159
Conor Gearty / Noel Monahan	162
Sheridan Clan	163
Plants of Granard area	164
Trades and Businesses in Granard - late 1800's - 1980's	165
Granard in the new Millennium	178
Sources	179
Index	181
Acknowledgements	184

Coat of Arms and Motto of Town of Granard

The Motte of Granard is represented by the green height resulting from dividing the shield per chevron. The *Ear of Corn* and the *Flax Stalk* represent Granard's longstanding as a market town. The *Harp* recalls the part played by Granard as a centre for the cultivation of that instrument.

The Coat of Arms and Motto were designed and recorded in Dublin Castle in May 1981.

Introduction

A veritable treasure house of history, Granard and its environs is justly proud of its past. Mindful of our heritage and the obligation to help perpetuate it, a local history group was formed in the I.C.A. Guild in 1986. Nine members met regularly over twelve months to study, discuss and edit a wealth of material. Each section was researched and written by a different member. The research entailed visits to the National Library, delving into old parish registers, photography, sketching and interviewing older residents who were more than willing to talk of times past.

At the beginning of the year 2002, the idea of compiling further information about the area was considered by members of the Guild. News that the long anticipated archaeological dig at Granardkill was to commence encouraged us to continue further research to add to the original edition of this book. We are privileged to include a detailed account of "The Dig" at Granardkill. The 150th anniversary of the Great Hunger stimulated further research. Fragments of information were found which helped to put together a clearer picture of that tragic time in Granard Union Workhouse. A local resident compiled a fascinating directory charting, from the early 18th century, the householders of the town and their varied occupations. A young graduate from Granard graciously shared with us her expertise in cartography, which helped to reinforce an overall view of the area in both written and visual terms. Other substantial and interesting material was also made available.

The Guild members were greatly encouraged by the sponsorship and co-operation from Longford Community Resources Limited (LCRL). The project went ahead and has further increased the treasure store of "Granard its History our Heritage".

Original Local History Group, 1987: Joy Burns; Sheila Donoghue; Margot Gearty; Caro Gillooly; Bernadette Grier; Elizabeth McGahern; Peggie O'Reilly; Elizabeth Regan (RIP); Rose Sheridan.

Sub-committee, 2002: Joy Burns; Mai Fanning; Patti Fitzgerald; Roseanne Garland; Margot Gearty; Bernadette Grier; Bridie McMahon; Maura Sheridan.

Editors: Joy Burns and Bernadette Grier.

History of Granard

The two distinctive features of Granard's skyline are the octagonal spire of St. Mary's Church and the massive mound of the Motte. This latter gives a clue to the town's antiquity. Granard's cultural heritage forms a fascinating complex tapestry, the threads of which can be traced back to the dawn of history.

The name 'Granard' is an adaptation of an older pre-Gaelic name 'Granaret' or 'Granaruid', the precise definition of which time has obscured. We can choose between such varied meanings as "The hill of the sun", "The hill of the grain" or "Ugly height". The topography of the area gives support to each definition.

Granard in the Prehistoric Era

The early inhabitants of Ireland migrated inland by sea, river or lake in search of food. Recently the lake shore at Lough Kinale (see Special Features) is giving up its secrets and showing tentative signs of an early settlement there, probably a hunting camp belonging to the close of the Mesolithic era when survival was the name of the game.

The neolithic people were farmers who cultivated the soil and had domestic animals. They also raised massive stone structures. The only stone circles in the midlands are the two at Granard (see Special Features). These stones give mute testimony to there being a considerable population here in 3000 to 1500 B.C.

The Dawn of History

Granard would have had its cattle-raiding, slave-owning chieftain. His rath could have been sited where the remains of a rath can be seen in a field opposite Granardkill old Church where the original town of Granard was sited.

Although ringforts have not escaped the ravages of progressive farming about 90 are recorded for the Granard area.

The crannog was another type of dwelling from this era and the crannog in Derragh Lake has given miscellaneous stone age items to the National Museum. The curious black bog oak hut at Aughamore may yet be proven to date from this time.

Traces of 'Druidism rites' linger on in the place name of the townland of Tonnyfubble (see Place Names).

Granard's importance can be gauged by the fact that it is mentioned many times in various annals though often only to record a battle or the death of a chieftain.

Tigerach, Abbot of Clonmacnoise and also the Four Masters record that at Granard in 236 "the tenth year of Cormac, the Battle of Granard was fought between Cormac the grandson of Conn and the Ulstermen this year." The Black Pig's Dyke may have been used as the boundary line of an impregnable line of defence. As a result of the battle at Granard the men of Ulster were driven from their province into the Isle of Man and the Hebrides.

Eochaid Aireamh, an ancient High King had a daughter called Teathba to whom he gave some territory. "It was from the noble maiden the entire region got its name."

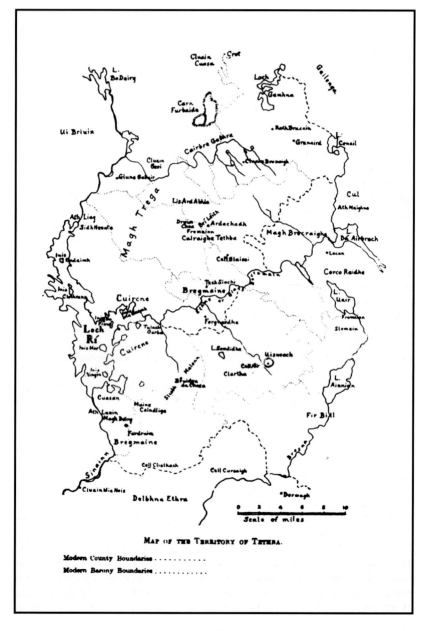

MAP OF THE TERRITORY OF TETHBA.

Modern County Boundaries . . . .
Modern Barony Boundaries . . . .

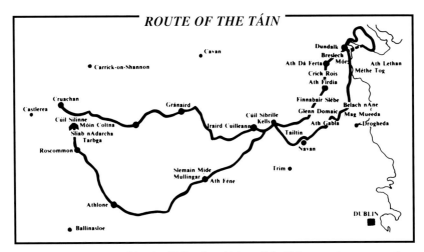

ROUTE OF THE TÁIN

The Annals record in the Táin that "they (Madb's army) went on then and spent the night in Granard in North Teathba. Fergus sent a warning from there to the men of Ulster because of old friendship. Fergus was then given the head of the army out in front of the troops. He made a great detour southwards to give Ulster time to gather an army together." (— Táin — translated by Thomas Kinsella.)

Niall of the Nine Hostages, King of Tara 379 – 406, established two of his sons in Teffia, dividing it into North and South. Cairbre took the supremacy of North Teffia which included the Granard area. The people living there were called the Glasraidhe – descendants of the early inhabitants. Cairbre Gabhra was the name attached to North Teffia during the period of its subjection by Cairbre and his descendants.

St. Patrick
St. Patrick's arrival in the 'dark land of Northern Teathba' is well documented in The Annals. Cairbre – son of Niall of the Nine Hostages was then Chieftain though absent at the time of St. Patrick's visit. His sons gave Patrick a charming site *(locus amoenus)*. Here he ordained Gusacht and founded a Church. This apparently developed into a monastic site. The Annals record that in 765 "Fiachra of Granard, presumably the Abbot, died". Regretfully no High Cross or Round Tower marks the place but the spirit of the Saint's message lives on.

Battles at Granard
In 476 "the eighteenth of Oilioll. The battle of Granard by Eochaidh, son of Cairbre, son of Oilioll, son of Dunlaing, son of Enda Niadh, against the King of Leinster".

About the eighth century, while Úi Cairbre still ruled North Teabhtha, the area was invaded by people from Maghrein (modern South Leitrim). These were the Conmaicne. By the eleventh century they were the dominant people in the territory between the Shannon and the Inny giving their tribe name to the area. The Conmaicne had in the tenth century a chieftain named Anghail whose descendants became known as Úi Anghaile (Annaly) and they became the ruling clan. Both Conmaicne and Annaly had different territorial connotations at various times. The older name of Teffia was superseded by Annaly, a name given to the territory for about 600 years.

In 1069 (A.F.M.) "An army was led by Murchadh, son of Diarmuid (son of Mael-na-mbo) into Meath, where he burned territories and churches, namely Granard." Granard was burned again when in 1272 Aed O Conchobhain "like an angel of destruction passed through it and the neighbouring Meath."

The Viking and Norman Influence
At the Battle of Clontarf a grandson of Anghail earned himself the name of Fearghal — meaning valiant. He and his soldiers came westwards to where the meandering river Camlin looped to almost form a circle. To fortify this area completely he built ramparts. His headquarters became known as Longfort Úi Fearghail. Later it became the site of the present town of Longford. Fearghail's descendants were called O'Ferralls, O'Ferrell, Farrell, a chief named Braon being the first to adopt the surname in 1155 (A.F.M.)

The last of the Úi Cairbre chiefs 'Mac mhic Cronan' was slain in 1161 and the O'Farrells became chiefs of the Granard area. Moate Farrell was held to have been the inauguration mound of the O'Farrells, chiefs of Annaly.

Sketch of Motte and Bailey (see Special Features)

The repercussions of the Norman invasion were most definitely felt in this area. In 1176 the King of Conmacne submitted his title to Henry II and was restyled Lord of Anghaile (Annaly). O'Farrell thought he was secure in his lands but the district around Granard was granted by Hugh de Lacy to Richard de Tuite in the subinfeudation of Meath. To consolidate his position, de Tuite built his "motte on an existing height" in 1199. At that time he was reputed to "be the owner of 750 sheep".

In 1205 Richard de Tuite invited Cistercian monks from St. Mary's Abbey, Dublin, to found a monastery at Abbeylara. Eighteen cantreds of land were given — a cantred being ten tuatha c.f. Townlands. The jurisdiction of the Monastery extended to Granard and the vicarage of Granard was also called "St. Mary's".

On 12th August, 1210, King John visited the area. The following year Richard de Tuite was killed by a falling tower at Athlone and was buried in Abbeylara. In 1215 the castle of Granard was listed among those returned to Walter de Lacy (ref. Sweetman). On the death of de Lacy, Granard passed in 1241 to Geoffrey de Grenville who was married to Walter's granddaughter Matilda.

The Bruce Invasion

Granard's greatest disaster came in November, 1315 when Con O'Farrell refused to submit to Edward Bruce. A fierce battle lasting two days took place. The old walled town (at Granardkill) was eventually razed. The Book of Howth says: "About the feast of St. Tendrow (Andrew) the said Bruce did burn Kells in Mythe and Granard and did spoil the Abbey thereof".

The Bruce Invasion marks the decline of the power of the Normans. The major land-owning family were the de Verdens. As the de Verdens were represented by four infant heiresses this probably led to the collapse of the Norman occupation.

The medieval site of the town at Granardkill is believed to be the only one of its type in the country. When it was abandoned in 1315 the site was not affected by later buildings. It has yet to be excavated.

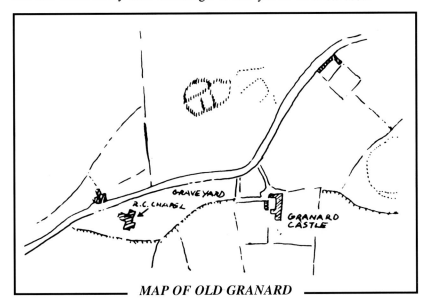

MAP OF OLD GRANARD

THE O'FARRELLS

In 1323 Donal O'Farrell defeated some English soldiers under their leader Bermingham in the townland of Killenawas (Soldiers' Wood). Tradition says that a section of O'Farrell's men concealed themselves in a wood at this place, hence the name.

In 1405 Granard became the chief seat of the O'Farrells of Upper Annaly (O'Farrell Bán) and Longford town the capital of Lower Annaly. William O'Farrell built a castle at Granard which was captured by the English in 1420. On their abandoning it, William demolished the castle for fear of their occupying it again. (A. Conn.)

In 1429 King henry VI gave a grant of £10 to his subjects to build castles 20 feet long, 16 feet wide and 40 feet high. These were called Tower houses. The four castles in Robinstown, Tully, Ballymore and Coolcor most likely were Tower houses.

In 1475 the chieftainship of Annaly was assumed by John O'Farrell in preference to his brother who was blind. The chief died at Granard after his inauguration and was buried in Abbeylara (A.F.M.).

In 1479-80 the Irish Parliament exacted a statute forbidding English merchants from having any contact with the market recently set up by the Irish at Granard as it was doing harm to the English markets of Meath. Thus it would appear that by the late 15th century Granard was an important settlement of the Irish at Anghaile.

THE BARONY

On 27th April, 1576 the Lord Deputy Sir Henry Sidney wrote: "As to Annalye or O'Ferralla country — (it) was made shire ground by me by the name of County Longford."

In the first year of his reign, King James I established an Inquisition to sit in Granard on 10th January. The King claimed that all lands, tenancies and hereditments reverted to the Crown. The Inquisition at Ardaghe on 4th April 1612 legally defined the county boundaries beginning "in a small stream at Ballywillan". Longford was divided into six Baronies. The Barony of Granard was formed from (a) Territory of Clanshane — Granard, Abbeylara, Colmcille, (b) Territory of Slewcarberie, Dromard, Colmcille. Granard Barony had an area of 139¼ Cartrons. The word cartron was applied to a piece of land varying from 60 – 160 acres.

By 1586 English control must have been established as in that year the site of the manor of Granard was leased by the Crown to Roger Radford. In 1593 the manor and parsonage which had been recovered from the O'Farrells were leased to Sir Francis Shane, Sir Francis Aungier, W. Plunkett, James Nugent and others.

William Nugent, 5th son of the 14th Lord Delvin, lived at Killasonna in this period. He was grandfather of Sir Ignatius Nugent who was knighted by the Emperor Charles VI and ancestor of Christopher James

Count Nugent. In 1596 William took and burned the Castle at Cowlecorr (Coolcor).

The Baronies of Longford

St. Patrick's Hospital between 1553 and 1612
It is known that a hospital existed in the area from two references made in 1595 and 1612 (Gwynn and Hadcock, Ir. Record Comm. 1830 – 213). "In 1612 in the reign of James I the King made a lease to Richard Hardinge Esq. in the Anelie one ruinous Church, 3 messuages 40a. arable and 30 pasture parcel of the lands of the hospital of St. Patrick called Granardkille in O'Farrell's country . . . the moiety of the tithes of Granard Rectory . . . parcel of the estate of the abbey of Granard. The north cartron of Leitrim near Drohednagalliagh . . . half of the cartron of Bealmore; a small millhead and site of the Windmill near Granardkill . . . the tithes of 4 granges near Granard including the Grange of Rincoll or Ricoole, parcel of the late Monastery of the Blessed Virgin of Larag otherwise Learah or Granard. The castle, town and lands of Granard Shehan alias Cartron Caslane, Racronan and Teemore with their appurtances."

CHARTER OF JAMES I
In 1612 James I granted to Sir Francis Shane "some annual fairs at Granard" while in both 1618 and 1620 Sir Francis Aungier received grants of a market and two fairs. Fairs and markets could only be held on charter from the King. A charter was granted to the individuals who were responsible for the organisation of the fair, for settling disputes and for providing a site. In return they collected tolls on animals and produce sold at fairs.

GRANARD AS A MILITARY BASE
Granard's geographical position places it in the path of an army on the march north-south and so the area many times suffered the turbulence of war. During the rebellion of 1641 when Owen Roe O'Neill's army was in nearby Co. Cavan, he "collected provisions for his army by setting fire to a bull to whose lowing all the kine of the Granard district assembled". During the Confederate War Granard became an important military base for James Touchet, Earl of Castlehaven, who was in command of the Leinster Cavalry. His adversary, Robert Monroe, approaching from the north, encountered "Myles the Slasher" and his men at the Bridge of Finea. A fierce battle ensued before Castlehaven eventually arrived to save this strategic place.

The importance of Granard as a military base was recognised from earliest times. When an extensive barrack building programme was undertaken in the late 1690s Granard was number one in the original scheme. Although the town was then situated in Granardkill, the site chosen for the barracks was at Cartronwillan Lane, close to the site of the present barracks. Gradually the old town was abandoned and the new town grew up principally on the townland of Rathcronan. The only remaining traces of old Granard are 'hillocks' in the field opposite the cemetery in Granardkill.

Further land confiscation took place after the Cromwellian invasion (1657) – "all those who got land in Longford were soldiers". The whole nation was declared guilty of rebellion. There were 29 confiscations of papist proprietors in the Barony of Granard — 17 of whom were O'Farrells. Their land was valued at £600 per 1,000 acres. They were given land in South Clare provided each claimant could prove his good conduct during the ten years war and satisfy the Revenue Commissioners in Athlone as to the quality of his lands. A dispossessed papist might choose instead to become a Tory and remain in hiding in the woods, sharing the lot of the wolf and the priest — that of being hunted for the price on his head. It is not recorded if there were any Granard girls among the hundreds of those who were transported to the sugar plantations of Barbados and Jamaica. The census of 1659 shows a population of 1,482 in the Barony.

THE BOROUGH OF GRANARD
1678
Charles II granted a Charter to the town to return two members of Parliament. Two members were returned until the Act of Union.

"*Charles the second by the Grace of God of God of England Scotland ffrance & Ireland King Defender of the ffaith &c To all to whom these presents shall come Greeting .... the present ffreehoulders within the said towne of Granard as those which att any tyme hereafter shall be made by the said ffrances Earle of Longford his heires & assnes shall & may have full power & authority by the major parte of the voices of the said freehoulders bee present in the said towne att the tyme of Ellecčon to choose re-turne & send two discreete Burgesses to serve for the towne of Granard unto every Parliament ....att Dublin the foure & twentyeth day of August in the Thirtyeth yeare of our Reigne.*

Penal Times
The Penal Laws may not have been so rigidly enforced as Granard had a registered priest — James Reilly — and an assistant priest who was also a doctor — Father Fergus Lee (1673 – 1745). A large stone in the townland of Ballynagall is referred to as the Mass Rock.

GRANARD'S MUSICAL HERITAGE

In the early part of the century O'Carolan, one of Ireland's leading composers visited the area. It is presumed that he stayed in Castlenugent House (now the home of the Smyth family). Here he composed one of his well known tunes "Grace Nugent" for the unmarried daughter of the house. In 1720/21 "on a fair Sunday morning" while on his way to Mass in Granardkill, O'Carolan met Miss Fetherston and after some witty conversation between the blind harper and the charming lady he composed music and verse entitled "Miss Fetherston" or "O'Carolan's Devotion". English was the medium used in deference to Miss Fetherston's lack of Irish.

Although it was still Penal times all was not doom and gloom in Granard. In 1781 the first ever Irish music festival was held for harpers in the town. The festival was sponsored by John Dungan, a successful Granard exile living in Copenhagen. Charles Fanning won the first prize of ten guineas for his playing of "An Coolin"; Arthur O'Neill was second and Rose Mooney third. A second Ball (festival) was held in June 1782 and a third in 1785.

A first-hand account of the Balls (as the festivals were called) was recorded by Arthur O'Neill. He described the third ball as "The greatest ever Irish National Ball, respecting Irish Harps ever held in this country." John Dungan, Patron, Lord and Lady Longford and over a thousand others attended the event.

In this period the Borough of Granard was the joint property of Mrs. McCartney and Mrs. Greville.

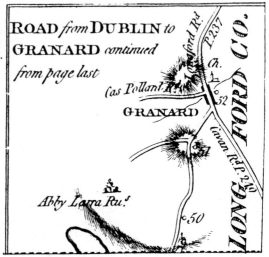

This map, published in 1778 by George Taylor and Andrew Skinner, gives an idea of the layout of the town at the time of the first Harp Festival.

1798
"The Year of the French" saw large numbers from different creeds including many men of property becoming United Irishmen. Their names live on in the Roll of Honour – Patrick and Henry O'Connell of Cranary; O'Keefe of Ballinlough; Patrick Farrell of Ballinree; while the Protestants included Alexander Crombie of Leitrim, Granard. Hans and Alex Denniston of Prospect, Rathbracken who were also Officers in the Yeomanry Corps of Mostrim.

When Humbert landed in Killcummin near Killala, Hans Denniston went to Belfast to consult with the northern directorate of the United Irishmen. On 3rd September Humbert left Castlebar and Hans arrived back with the proposal to attack and occupy Granard. The Commander of the Barracks despatched messengers to Cavan for reinforcements and a forced night march brought Major Cottingham and 100 men to the town. About 9 o'clock the insurgents approached Cottingham's men. The insurgents broke into three columns: the column on the left charged towards the Motte to eliminate the signalling station on the top. They were caught in cross fire and the traces of bullet holes are still to be seen in St. Patrick's Church. The centre column advanced driving cattle ahead of them but they were routed by a cavalry charge. The column on the right attacked the Barracks, gained entrance, and it was here that the main battle was fought lasting five hours. O'Farrell and the O'Connells were killed and this had a disheartening effect on the insurgents, who retreated. Many escaped down Tuite's Lane.

Tuite's Lane.

Photo: Ian White.

The Dennistons and O'Keefe also evaded being captured. "The slaughter that ensued was great" is recorded in Major Cottingham's despatch.

Dublin Caſtle, *8th September*, 1798.

A Body of Inſurgents having collected near *Granard*, on *Wedneſday* laſt, ſeveral Yeoman Corps in the Neighbourhood, and from the County of *Cavan*, commanded by Captain *Cottingham*, collected with Celerity, and entirely defeated the Inſurgents at the Town of *Granard*, killing about One Hundred and Fifty, and diſperſing the Remainder. The Yeomanry experienced no Loſs.

On the ſame Evening Lord *Longford*, at the Head of a Body of Yeomanry, aſſiſted by a Detachment of the King's Troops, attacked a Body of Rebels at *Wilſon's Hoſpital*, and put them to Flight, with much Slaughter.

One hundred and fifty rebels were hanged near the base of the Motte. Hempenstall – "the walking Gallows" acted as "judge, jury and hangman". Their bodies were thrown into the quarry near the site of the Catholic Church, later to be re-interred when the Church and a new lane were being constructed. For five years rebels were on the run but a papist rebel, Patrick Gilchrist, was successfully concealed by the Master of the Masonic Hall. (see Folklore).

ACT OF UNION
On the 22nd February 1800 the Earl of Granard protested against the Act of Union, but the Act was passed, with the help of the two representatives from Granard – Fulk Greville and G. Fulk Littleton, and Granard Borough lost its elective franchise.

"THE THRASHERS"
1806/7

During this period an illegal secret oath-bound organisation called "The Thrashers" was active in the area. The members wore white shirts and white handkerchiefs on their heads when they went to intimidate people. Though mostly Catholics, they opposed "the tithes paid to Roman Catholic Clergy and the rates and prices of manual and manufacturing labour". The movement ended when four of its members were sentenced to be twice whipped publicly in Granard and imprisoned for six months. Their leader, Peter Morris, was hanged.

TOWN AND COUNTRY DWELLINGS
1809/1837

The main part of the existing town dates from this era (see Street Signs). This included a wide thoroughfare suitable for busy market days and fairs. Residential areas, some with domed arches, branched off Barrack Street and Main Street. The survey of 1837 shows the number of houses per street: Main Street (88); Market House Road (56); Moxham Street (36); The Hill (64); Tuite's Lane (14); Water Lane (9). The Ball Alley had 46 houses, one of which had a "rope walk". Other lanes were Porter's Row; Silver Street, The Diamond, Smith's Lane and Gortawillan Lane.

A cabin which can still be seen in the townland of Aughnagarron is reputed to date from this era. It is thatched, mudwalled and has a wicker chimney.

The following large houses in the Granard area were listed in Lewis Topography in 1837: Some of the houses are still inhabited.

Clonfin House – Residence of J. Thompson
Mossvale, Ferskill – Residence of J. Barton
Cartroncar House – Residence of J. W. Bond

Moor Hill House. *Photo: E. Mullaney.*

Moorhill House — Residence of R. Blackhall
Bessville — Residence of C. Helden
Castle Nugent — Residence of W. Webb
Higginstown — Residence of F. Tuite
Springpark, Coolarty
Spring Villa, Coolarty

The Gate Lodge, Clonfin House, residence of the Thompsons. In 1824 Major Thompson was Seneschal in Granard. The house was described in 1837 as a handsome residence, pleasantly situated in a well cultivated demesne which included 30 acres of oakwood. *Photo: Ian White.*

Rockfield House, Dalystown — Residence of Lawrence P. Reynolds, J.P.
Ballinlough House – Edward Irwin
Toneen Lodge
Killasonna House.

Castlenugent House. *Photo: R.W. Stafford.*

Daniel O'Connell
When Daniel O'Connell was organising the Catholic Emancipation Movement, Longford responded to his Catholic Association Rent plan. The last Sunday of the month was fixed as the day for its collection (one penny). Granard sent in its contribution on 25th January, 1824. At a county meeting in September 1825, the Chairman was John C. Nugent of Killasonna.

J. D. Brady, Springtown, Granard, declared at a meeting that "The Catholics came to Parliament to seek our rights – not to deprive our neighbours of theirs."

In August, 1827, Daniel O'Connell came to Longford town and successfully defended Fr. E. McGaver in a case over a disputed will. Fr. McGaver P.P. of Granard was a keen local activist for O'Connell.

Granard in the 1830s
The agricultural depression and the collapse of the linen trade in the 1820s and 1830s resulted in large numbers of destitute people. A cholera outbreak in Granard in 1832 caused a Board of Health to be set up, which got £100 from Central Funds to help relieve the severe poverty. They sought and obtained from central funds the sum of £100 as it proved impossible to raise more than £6 locally. Their plea for £100 was reinforced by a Dr. Sergeant who was sent to inspect the area from headquarters. "No house into which I called to visit a cholera patient since my arrival in this town did I see a bedstead, or anything in the shape of a bed better than a bundle of half wet straw separated from the pig-stye by a row of loose stones, but the inmates are in the most abject misery." In 1835 an "Examination" was held to make enquiries into the living conditions in the area. The persons who attended the "Examination" were: Mr. Peter Corcoran, grocer and general retailer; Mr. Kirwan, M.D.; Patrick Maguire, day-labourer; Mr. Montgomery, churchwarden; Thomas Moxham, farmer; Mr. J. Murtagh, cloth merchant; Rev. Mr. Robinson, Rector and J.P.; Rev. M. Sheridan, J.P., and Mr. Thompson, J.P.

They reported that the wages for female field workers varied between 3d or 4d a day for a few weeks in spring and harvest. Due to the decline of the linen trade spinners paid 7d for a pound of dressed flax. "When they have spun it into two hanks, which occupies two days, they receive 8d for it."

A great portion of the male labourers were without work in the winter. Their summer wage was 10d a day without food, the winter wage 6d to 8d. Their diet in winter was potatoes and salt or salt herrings. In summer they had a "scanty supply of potatoes and milk".

The town was described as having no almshouse or fever hospital, though there was a dispensary. Such was the state of the parish (and many other parishes) when the Government drew up a Relief Scheme – The Poor Law Act 1838. Ireland was divided into 120 Poor Law Unions, (Unions of Parishes).

Granard Union Workhouse

A workhouse was built at a central place in each Union and was governed by a Board of Guardians. They had the right to strike a rate and use the money to support the workhouse.

Foundation Stone of Granard Workhouse. *Photo: Alison Burns.*

Granard Union included parts of Co. Longford, Cavan and Westmeath. Included in the Union were the parishes of Granard, Clonbroney, Gelshagh, Colmcille, Castlenugent, Abbeylara, Lough Gowna, Scrabby, Mullaghoran, Drumlummun, Fore, Streete, Rathowen and half of Coole. There were seven ex-officio guardians and 21 elected guardians. The population of the Union in 1831 was 52,152.

The Workhouse was contracted for on 4th November 1840. The contractor was Mr. Kelly, Ballinacross. It cost £5,925 for buildings, £1,225 for fittings and occupied an area of 6 acres, 1 rood, 20 perches, purchased for £350. The building was completed on 4th February 1842 with accommodation for 600 persons — though this was inadequate. It was self-contained, having a Church, Church of Ireland Chapel, Infirmary, School and Bakery. The regime was unattractive with a diet of porridge, potatoes, salt and buttermilk. The system of splitting families was heart-rending. Children wore numbers on their backs in order to be identified. Famine stalked when the potato crop failed. Extra accommodation was found in huts at the boundary walls of the workhouse; also at Beltons of Ballinlough and at Springlawn House. Patients were collected by horse drawn wagons from the outlying areas.

Personnel

In 1870 the Chairman of the Board of Guardians was James Dease D.L.; Master of Workhouse – James Lee; Matron – Ann Kiernan; Protestant Chaplain – Rev. Thos. W. Green; Roman Catholic Chaplain – Rev. Edward McGaver; Clerk to the Board of Guardians – William Higgins; Medical Officer – vacant; Schoolmaster – Bernard Farrell; Schoolmistress – Margaret Mahon; Relieving Officers – Eugene Doherty, Granardkill, and Dillon O'Reilly, Kilcogy.

The Workhouse eventually closed in 1932. Some of the families were rehoused in Columcille Terrace.

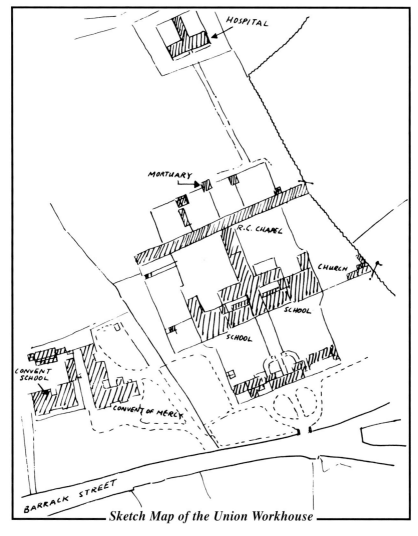

Sketch Map of the Union Workhouse

Famine Times

The Granard area escaped the worst ravages of the famine so numerous "knights of the road" (riderí an Bhóthair) came to the town for shelter and food. Many of them were typhus carriers and so the three-storey high fever hospital was built. In return for a night's lodgings, work had to be done which often included the digging of the pauper's grave in "Bully's Acre" opposite Carra Church. It is no surprise that the Parliamentary Gazeteer of 1846 records that the town "is not in an improving condition". 1847 was indeed 'black' for Granard. Lord Greville of Clonhugh, Mullingar, local landlord, recorded in his diary that in 1847 the Board of Guardians of Granard Workhouse asked to be dissolved as they were "convinced they faced bankruptcy". They were not allowed to do so but advised instead to insist on the "recovery of the rates".

The Bishop's letter reports -
Ballymahon,
19 May 1847

Very Rev. Dr. Cullen, Rector, Irish College, Rome

. . . We have in this Diocese five poor houses and the average deaths in the week are beyond 100 persons in each. . . Fever, dysentery and starvation are everywhere. God alone can see the end.

Yours etc.
+ W. Higgins

On 6th October 1847 Rev. William Dawson died of a fever "caught in the discharge of his duties". He is buried in Granardkill.

Relief works carried out during the famine included the improvement of the New Road (Market Street) and lowering of inclines.

(See Folklore)

THE ELECTION OF 1870

Two years prior to the passing of the Secret Ballot Act, John Martin, brother-in-law of John Mitchell, stood for election against the local landlord, Greville. The limited franchise meant that the electors were all landowners. They had to openly declare their vote knowing that to vote for one candidate could later lead to reprisals, while to vote for the other could even mean eviction. In a hotly contested election Martin was defeated.

FAMINE STRIKES AGAIN
1879
The potato crop fails once more and the emigrant songwriter laments "Come back to Erin when the Champions grow". Famine and emigration have taken their toll as the census of 1881 shows a decline of population in the Barony to 16,931, a decrease of over 32% since 1831.

End of 19th Century

An active branch of Michael Davitt's Land League was formed. Members erected a "house of sods" in Ballymacrolly for an evicted family.

Parnell held a mass meeting in a field opposite the present Cattle Mart. Tim Michael Healy was the Member of Parliament for the Granard area from 1887 until 1891.

The "Parnell Split" brought disunity to the town. The coming together of the '98 Centenary Club helped to heal the breach as did the United Irish League which was formed by William O'Brien. This League got considerable amount of support in the area, and in 1918 its adherents joined the Sinn Féin movement.

Admissions Workhouse, Granard. *Photo: Sister Maeve Brady.*

Troubled Times

From 1917 – 1922 Michael Collins, one of the principal founders of the State, was a frequent visitor to Granard. He came to visit his fiancée, Kitty Kiernan, Greville Arms Hotel.

It was in the Greville Arms Hotel, owned by the Kiernan family, that the District Inspector, Philip St. John Howlett Kelleher from Macroom was shot on 31st October 1920, "as there was a case against him". Father Butler, C.C., Granard, attended Kelleher. Father Butler later recalled the regret felt by the people of Granard when they attended the funeral service which took place outside the hotel. Several people from the town were interrogated afterwards in Longford Barracks.

Retaliation for the D.I.'s death was swift and severe. By the 3rd November, most of the inhabitants of the town had already fled, some having time only to "bring a bundle of blankets". At 11.30p.m., 11 lorries crammed with Black and Tans and Auxiliaries roared into the town. Fourteen houses in all were burned. L. D. Kiernan's Spirit and Grocery establishment; M. Kiernan's Hardware Department; The Greville Arms Hotel; Market House; P. Heslin's Grocery, Bar and Steam Bakery; J. Cosgrove's Grocery; M. Kelly's Grocery and Bar; Messrs B. Mackens; J. W. Burns; J. Kellets; Mrs. Grehans; Mrs. Pettit's Grocery, Bar and Hardware premises; F. Majors; P. O'Hara's Grocery and Bar; M. J. Tierney's Drapery Store; T. O'Reilly's. Messrs. Markey's, Doherty's and Kelly's business houses had their fires promptly extinguished. Prompt action by Messrs. Deacon, Irwin and Lennox saved other houses from a similar fate. Kiernan's property and the adjacent Market House were special targets. Pettit's shop smouldered for weeks as the cellars contained a supply of soap and candles for the Workhouse.

The Burning of Granard. *Photo: Courtesy National Museum.*

Clonfin Ambush

Those were the troubled times when "the lamps of Granard streets were left to quench in their own death-like way". There was another light not so easily quenched: Sean McEoin, who was born in Ballinlough and known as "The Blacksmith of Ballinalee", was an inspiration to the men of his home town. It was he, with his Flying Column of 20 men, who at 3.00p.m. on 2nd February 1921 successfully ambushed a contingent of Auxiliaries at Clonfin on the Ballinalee Road. Tom Brady, Longford Road, the last surviving member of the Column, recalls the "great satisfaction" felt by them in Bracken Wood when they were all re-united in victory.

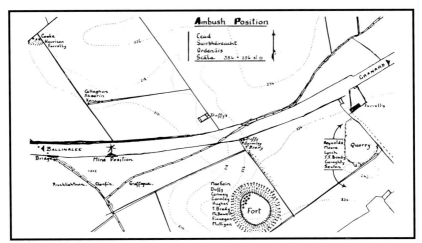

Names of those who participated in the Clonfin Ambush

Sean McEoin (in command)
Sean Duffy (2nd in command)
Seamus Conway
Hugh Hourican
Paddy Finnegan
Mick Mulligan
Michael F. Reynolds
Jim Sheeran
Tom Brady
Mick Gormley
Larry Geraghty

Pat Cooke
John Moore
James J. Brady
Jack Hughes
John McDowell
Mick Kenny
Paddy Callaghan
Sean Sexton
James Farrelly
Paddy Lynch

This Memorial to the men who took part in the Ambush can be seen at Clonfin on the road from Granard to Ballinalee.

Photo: Ian White.

In February 1923 the Military Barracks was burned but was later rebuilt on the same site as a Garda Barracks. Granard was rebuilt and resumed its popularity as a market town.

1949

On 13th October 1949 a branch of the Irish Countrywomen's Association was founded and the Guild continued to flourish with members from the town and the surrounding rural area.

Harp Festival Revival

1981 was a milestone in the history of Granard when the bi-centenary of the first Harp Festival was celebrated. This has now become an annual event and the Market House resounds yet again to the music of O'Carolan. The pageantry, traditional music and instrument making evoke memories of Granard's colourful and industrious past; a rich heritage which is proudly treasured.

Harp Festival Revival 1781–1981. *Photo: C. Gillooly.*

Town Commissioners

Granard had its Municipal Boundaries prescribed under the Municipal Boundaries Act of 1840. "From the Mote of Granard (1) situated on a commanding hill at the Western Extremity of the principal Street, in a Western direction, by a straight line to the Point (2) in the Road leading to the Roman Catholic Chapel, from whence a Lane leads into the Lower Road from Longford; thence along the said lane, passing the School-House and Glebe to the Longford Road at the Point (3) where the road from Bonlaghy enters it; thence in a straight line, North-easterly, to the Northern and highest Point of a remarkable Knoll (4), called "The Rocks", about One hundred yards Eastward of the Road from Scraby — thence in a straight line in a South-easterly direction to the square Boundary Stone (5) marked with a Broad Arrow on each face, near the North-eastern Angle of the Barrack Wall; thence in a straight line to the North-west Angle of the Garden Wall, belonging to Mr. Faulkner (6) thence in an Easterly direction to the fork of the roads leading to Cavan and Dublin (7); thence in a straight line South-westerly to a House belonging to, and now in occupation of, a man named Stratford in the Road from Street, about One hundred and Fifty Yards South of the Point at which the Edgeworthstown Road enters it (8); thence in a straight line to the Point first described." H. Pooley.

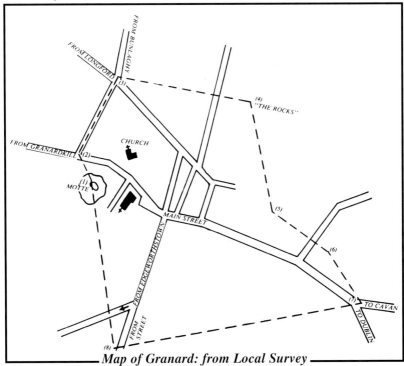

Map of Granard: from Local Survey

Urban councillors were established under the 1854 Town Improvement Act. They were responsible for supplying public services such as special housing, water supply, public lighting and sanitary facilities, road sweeping etc. In return they collected rents and rates and later tolls. On 3rd May, 1893 the Granard Urban Commissioners were:

Patrick M. O'Reilly, Chairman	Michael Drum, J.P.
Francis Reilly	Charles Brady
James Cosgrove	Michael Kelly
John McGovern	James Burns
John Nugent	

The Commissioners purchased the Lyttleton Moiety and the Greville Moiety for £600. This included the Fair Green, Pound, Butter Market, Corn Market, Market and Courthouse, "with the rights of holding fairs and markets in the manor of Granard and receiving the Fair and Market tolls".

As Granard was an Urban Council prior to the 1898 Government Act "It failed to have the advantages as to the agricultural grant re rates and County Cess." Hence in the 1920s and 1930s the Council was beset by financial difficulties. It found that it could not develop the services unless more rates were collected.

On 10th January 1941, Mr. Patrick Francis Patten, Malahide, was appointed by the Minister for Local Government and Public Health to take over the duties of the District Council. On 1st April, 1944 the Urban District Council was dissolved and replaced by Town Commissioners. The responsibility for most of the public services then rested with Longford County Council.

A view of the Motte.   *Photo: Ian White.*

Street Names

MAIN STREET

Turn of the Century. *Photo: Courtesy of National Museum.*

Present day Main Street. *Photo: A. Corcoran.*

MARKET STREET: (New Road) Cornmarket area.
MURPHY TERRACE: Patrick Murphy shot during Civil War – buried in Carra.
O'CALLAGHAN TERRACE: Patrick O'Callaghan, a member of the North Longford Flying Column.
WATER LANE: Site of O'Hara's Well – overflow forms the Camlin River.

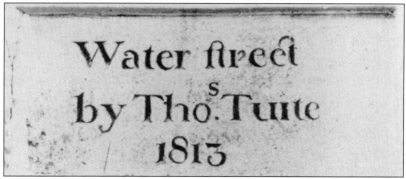

Photo: R.W. Stafford.

O'CARROLL TERRACE: Fr. O'Carroll C.C., killed in a car accident in 1952.
FARRELL TERRACE: 'Big Pat' was killed in the Battle of Granard 1798.
DENNISTON PARK: Two brothers were leaders in 1798.
TUITE'S LANE: The Norman family who were overlords of the area.
MILL'S LANE: James and Sarah Mills taught in the school attached to the Established Church.
ST. COLMCILLE'S TERRACE: Named after the Saint who is associated with Inishmore Monastery in Lough Gowna.
BALL ALLEY: So called as it had been the practice shot area for the army and also the game of handball was played at the gables of some of the houses. In 1924 a 'lighted coal' from a thatcher's pipe was the cause of a fire which burned the ten two-storied thatched houses. A small plantation now grows on the site.
MOXHAM STREET: Originally a French Huguenot family. Worked as carters; owned property and land.

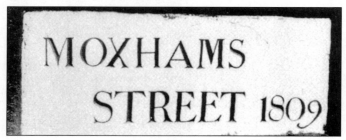

Photo: R.W. Stafford.

Photo: Ian White.

PARNELL ROW: Charles Stewart Parnell addressed a meeting in this area. Sir John Parnell was Parliamentary Representative for Granard in the 18th century.
CARTRONWILLAN LANE: An Anglo-Norman term for land and a mill – most likely a windmill.
REDMOND TERRACE: Named after John Redmond M.P., Leader of the Irish Parliamentary Party.
ST. PATRICK'S TERRACE
ST. JOSEPH'S ROAD
CHURCH VIEW.

Confessional Stone & Sacred Heart Statue, Church View.

Photo: Ian White.

BARRACK STREET

Old and New Barracks also Garda Residence. *Photo: Sr. Maeve Brady.*

Public Lighting

Oil lamps had been a feature of the town until 1926. The previous year, William Humphrey, a native of Mohill, built a generating station on the site where the Community Centre now stands. The first testing of the electric light took place in the Convent of Mercy where a Bazaar was being held. Later the Town Hall was lit for the performance of a play by the local Dramatic Troupe. By Christmas 1926, the street oil lamps had been replaced by electric lighting and Granard was one of the first small towns in Ireland to have this facility.

Mr. Humphrey and his electricians continued to operate efficiently until 1932 when he sold the goodwill to the E.S.B.

Old Street Lamps on "The Hill".
Photo: Ian White.

Special Features

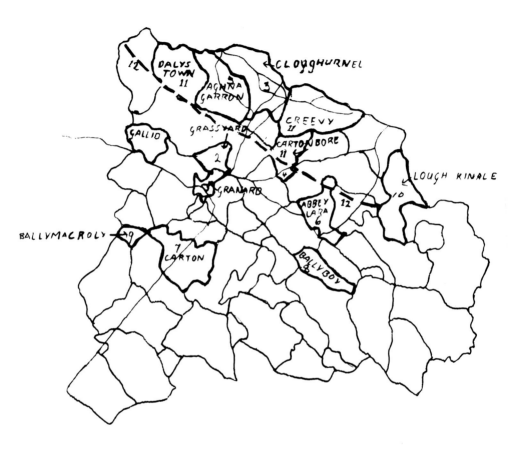

**Map of
Abbeylara and
Granard (part of)**

1. Motte
3. Stone Circle
5. Druid's Altar
7. St. Patrick's Well
9. Mill
11. Standing Stones

2. Carraig na h-Uaine
4. Stone Circle
6. St. Mary's Abbey
8. Tobar Rí an Domhnaigh
10. Louth Kinale – Book Shrine
12. Black Pig's Dyke

The Lough Kinale Shrine

This object, almost certainly a casket or shrine for a book, was found in the summer of 1986 on the bed of Lough Kinale, Co. Longford. Although it was in a dismantled state when found, most of its components survive and so the object can be almost completely reconstructed.

The Shrine is 34.5 cm. long, 28.0 cm wide, and measures 11.0 cm in thickness. Like most of the other surviving Irish book shrines it consists of a wooden box to which metal plates are nailed, the whole strengthened with tubular binding strips along the sides and corners.

The front is decorated with a series of cast and pierced mountings of bronze. The border consists of strips of tinned bronze ornamented with a continuous pattern of spirals, parts of the background being cut away to reveal a backing plate of differently-coloured bronze. The corners have oval mounts, set with coloured studs. A cross with cusped or concave arms embellished with a series of five cast bosses is the principal design. The bosses are decorated with scrollwork and each contains a coloured stud with an inlaid metal grille. The arms of the cross contain openwork panels of interlaced animals. Decorative discs with spiral ornaments also in openwork occur in the spaces between the arms.

The sides of the shrine are composed of sheets of tinned bronze to which are attached a series of medallions, each with animal heads projecting from the sides. There are three such medallions on the long sides — each bearing an openwork pattern of scrollwork and a coloured stud. Each short side bears a single medallion, fitted with a hinged loop which once contained a leather strap for carrying. The back plate is plain.

The shape and method of construction used in the Lough Kinale shrine is similar to other Irish book shrines. It is the earliest and largest example and the manuscript which it was made to contain would have been larger than the Book of Durrow, but smaller than the Book of Kells.

Although much of the decoration is still obscured, enough is visible to enable the shrine to be dated to the 8th century.

Lough Kinale

Lough Kinale (Loch Caoin Aoil, lake of fine limestone) is locally called Killina Lake, from a little hamlet of that name which was sited on the western shore. According to local tradition this village was submerged by the lake. There are two islands on the lake – Chapel Island and Bruree; "the former has the ruins of an old church on it; the latter is planted." *Lewis Top., 1837.*

Granard Motte. *Photo: A. Burns.*

The Motte

The Motte is a great flat topped earthen mound, on top of which would have been a timber tower surrounded by a palisade. Around the base was a U-shaped bailey, an enclosure surrounded by a palisade and ditch. Animals and soldiers were housed in the bailey. The Motte was sited "on an existing height", made higher by removing earth from the sides. It is the highest motte in Ireland, reputed to be 534 ft. above sea level. From this vantage point can be seen parts of nine counties, five lakes and the

faint outline of the Sliabh Bloom Mountains.
*"the view from the Motte
of Granáird over a tranquil
unrushed emptiness . . ."*

J. Montague
The Dead Kingdom

Stone Circles. *Photo: R.W. Stafford.*

Stone Circles

The above Stone Circle is situated three miles from Granard on the farm of Stephen Grier in the townland of Cloughernal. It consists of 24 stones, six being upright, seven placed on their sides and the remainder have fallen.

In the townland of Cartronbore the Circle originally consisted of 16 stones, two of which are erect and eight have fallen. These are the only examples of Stone Circles in the midlands.

Photo: R.W. Stafford.

Standing Stones

There are standing stones in the townlands of Creevy, Dalystown and Cartronbore. The word 'Gallid' as in townland means standing stone.

The Druid's Altar

There is a Cromlech or Dolmen (Stone Table) on the ordnance survey map of Aughnagarron. It now consists of one upright and two horizontal stones.

Carraig na h-Uaine

Carraig na h-Uaine: locally known as Carricknahoo or "The Rocks" or "Grainne's Cave". *Photo: R.W. Stafford.*

It is situated behind St. Colmcille's Terrace. The entrance to the 'cave' is now blocked. It is an interesting limestone reef knoll. The quarry at Ardgullion is also of geological interest.

Black Pig's Dyke

The Valley of the Black Pig or the Black Pig's Race or Dyke (Duncla) was the title given to the earthworks which in the 4th century formed the boundary between Ulster and the rest of the country. The builders also used the natural features of the land – lakes, bogs and forests as part of the defence.

The Dyke ran from Newry to the sea at Bundoran. In the Granard area it ran from Kinale lake to Lough Gowna. Traces are still to be seen in the townland of Ballinrud.

'A ridge of the Dunchaladh, the Black Pig's Dyke or Race
– the ancient frontier of Uladh'.

The Black Pig – J. Montague
(The Dead Kingdom)

Baker's Fort. *Photo: R.W. Stafford.*

Baker's Fort

Baker's Fort is off Main Street, behind A. Smith's shop. The Annals say that "In 1161, Matudan, grandson of Cronan, fell by the sons of McCongall at Granard." This may be the Cronan after whom the townland, Rathcronan, is named and the rath may have been the site of his residence.

The rath is now only 45 yards wide as part of it was demolished in 1924. The farmer discontinued the work as he considered it an unlucky omen when all his cattle died. The rath is probably called after a Mr. Baker who had a shop near the Bank of Ireland building.

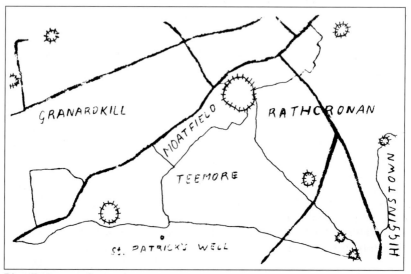

Ring Forts near Granard. *Sketch: Conor Murphy.*

Churches

Photo: Sr. Maeve.

St. Mary's Church

St. Mary's Church is built on a predominant height overlooking the town. The site of 3 roods 33 perches was granted by Richard Greville, the local landlord, to Bishop Kilduff, T. Pettit and Christopher Nugent.

The Church was designed by John Bourke, Dublin, at the request of Canon McGaver. The foundation stone was laid on Sunday, 8th September, 1860. The style is neo-Gothic, the plan cruciform. It was formally opened on 5th May, 1867, the preacher being Cardinal Cullen.

Twenty years later the tower and spire were built to complete the building and to house the 40 cwt. bell. The spire, which rises to a height of 170 feet, is topped by a medieval style cross 13 ft. high and has become a local landmark.

Priests have administered in Granard since the days of St. Patrick.

In the year 1608 John Gaffney, Vicar Apostolic, lived in Granard. A small chalice dated 1643 belonged to Fr. Heraty, Vicar of Granard.

11th July, 1704. Registration of priests at General Quarter Sessions of the Peace for County Longford: Rev. James Reilly, Ballybryan, aged 80. Ordained in 1661 at Paris by Dr. Edmund Reilly, Titular Archbishop of

Armagh. Sureties given by James Nugent, Castlenugent and Chris Dunleavy, Smear.
Rev. Fergus Lee, Castlenugent, aged 31. Ordained 1697. As he did not have sureties the registration was refused, but he remained as assistant priest and also practised as a doctor.
Rev. Owen Ruddy – name only survives.
Bishop Augustine Cheevers of Ardagh (1751 – 1756) resided with his niece Mrs. John Reilly, at Annville, Ballykilchrist.
Rev. Patrick Kiernan, Coolarty – see Commemorative Stone in Granardkille dated 1772. Died 1785.
Rev. Peter Daly; lived at Clough. Died 1816.
Rev. John Sheridan; died 1835.
Fr. Farrell Sheridan (nephew); died 1849.
Canon Edward McGaver; built St. Mary's. Died 1877.
Dean Nicholas O'Flanagan; died 1893.
Archdeacon James Smyth; died 1908.
Mons. Thomas Maguire; died 1923.
Canon Patrick Donohoe; died 1955.
Canon Denis O'Kane; died 1968.
Canon Thomas Sheeran, transferred after 13 months.
Canon Francis Gilfillan; died 1986.

Ticket.   *Courtesy: R. Monahan.*

St. Mary's Church – Original Interior.

St. Mary's Church – Modern Interior.

Photo: Sr. Maeve Brady.

The seven priests who were buried in the grounds of St. Mary's Church are:–
1. Canon Francis O'Farrell P.P. Clonbroney (died 1909).
2. Archdeacon Smith P.P. Granard (died 1908).
3. Rev. Eugene O'Reilly C.C. Granard (died 1900).
4. Monsignor Thomas Maguire P.P. Granard (died 1923).
5. Rev. Edward O'Carroll C.C. Granard (died 1952).
6. Dean O'Kane, Granard (died 1968).
7. Canon Francis Gilfillan (died 1986).

The Celtic Cross on far right marks the burial ground of nine Sisters of Mercy, Sacred Heart Convent, Granard. *Photo: Ian White.*

Church at Granardkill

A church was built in the latter part of the Penal Days and was situated in the graveyard at Granardkill. It is believed to have been the first slated

Oratory at Granardkille. *Photo: Sr. Maeve Brady.*

church in the Diocese. Ordinations by Bishop O'Higgins were held in the church in 1829 and 1831. The cemetery was consecrated in 1826. It was used as the Parish Church of Granard until 1867 when St. Mary's was built. Mass continued to be said there until 1961 when the church was demolished and a small oratory erected on the site.

St. Patrick's Church (C. of I.)

This site, close to the Motte, was originally the site of Catholic worship in Granard. The present building is thought to have been built in the early part of the 18th century. Various alterations including a belfry (before 1836) and restoration work have been made, the most recent being in 1980.

A Glebe House was built close to the Church in 1825 at a cost of £1015-7-8, it was a large two-storied house with basement. This was inhabited by the various Vicars of the Church until 1940 and demolished in 1959.

Interior of St. Patrick's Church. *Photo: R.W. Stafford.*

An Elegy on James Smith's Tomb
(In graveyard at St. Patrick's Church, Granard)

Here lies close by a tender mother's side
The father's darling hope, the sister's pride,
He fell full blossomed in the flower of youth
The noble pride of virtue, **worth** *and truth.*

Cold is the breast which early friendship warmed
Sunk is that form which each beholder charmed,
Silent that tongue, which pleaded for distress
Nerveless that hand, which used the poor to bless.

It's not this stone those virtues shall record
This but bespeaks a father's fond regard,
This last sad gift a parent could impart
The frail memorial of a bleeding heart.

This sad memorial of an only son
Whose accents could I hear them thus would run,
Grieve not my father, sisters do not weep
In Christ I trusted and in Christ I sleep.

Let this console you, that, but short my race
'Twas won with ardour and endowed with grace,
Removed above the view of mortal eyes
I sit with angels and enjoy the prize.

Learn hence frail youth, reflect ye sage
Youth well spent is more than Vestor's age.

Silverware

The flagon on the right, paten to the right and chalice in centre all bear the following inscription: –

In usum parochia Granardiensis Galielnio Brooke Vicario Annodomini 1766.

The chalice to the left and centre paten bear the inscription:

In usum sacellorum parochia de Granard Gulms Brooke vicario A.D. 1763.

The hallmarks indicate that they were made in Dublin. The paten to the left is E.P.N.S. and bears the inscription:

Granard Church 1842.

St. Patrick's Church.

Photo: Courtesy of the National Library of Ireland.

*Extracts from J. B. Leslie's Biographical Succession List, 1932
(M.S., R.C.B. Library)*

Ardagh Diocese
GRANARD
Vicars

1369 — Sir John Offyne	1737 — Samuel Span
1389/90 — Nemeas O'Sculaghan	1741 — Michael Neligan
1438 — Matthew Ycam	1761 — William Brooke
1438 — William Yfergayl	1805 — John Beresford
1438 — Matthew McAeda	1811 — Chrostopher Robinson
1438 — Eugene McMurceartayd	1838 — William Tomlinson
1441 — Wm. O'Fergail	1863 — Thomas Webb Green
1441 — Maurice MacGillarnean	1876 — Frederick Foster
1455 — Eugene McMuircertaig	1885 — Francis De Burgh Sidley
1455/56 — Wm. O'Fergayl	1914 — Arthur Reginald Burriss
1536/39 — Richard Wacfield (or Wakefield)	1926 — Edward Furlong
	1933 — Isaac Mayne
1552 — John Drover (Derver)	1934 — Hugh Maurice Daunt
1556/57 — Robert Nugent	1938 — Charles Richard Ryall
1610 — John Richardson	1941 — Cecil Maurice Kerr
1630 — William Smith	1966 — James Mansel Egerton Maguire
1661/62 — William Baylie	
1665 — John Ker	1978 — Robert Henderson
1702 — Essex Edgeworth	1983 — Thomas George Hudson

Methodist Church

This church was situated in Moxham Street. John Wesley visited Granard in 1758. In Crookshank's *History of Methodism* it states: "At Granard

Window of Methodist Church. *Photo: R.W. Stafford.*

he preached in the Barracks yard to a congregation and he had rarely in a new place seen one so much affected."

This building served the needs of the Catholic population from 1822 until St. Mary's was opened in 1867. The only remaining trace of the church is the ecclesiastical window.

Tully Presbyterian Church

This church was built for the needs of Presbyterian families in the townlands of Coolarty and Tully near Granard in 1855, on land owned by Mr. J. W. Bond. The Wilson-Slater family of Whitehall contributed substantially to the cost of the building. The church was in use up to the mid-1950s. The largest mullioned window was donated for use at the Friary, Multyfarnham and its pulpit to Malahide Presbyterian Church.

Tully Presbyterian Church. *Photo: W. Farrell.*

Lourdes Grotto

This grotto, situated beside St. Mary's Church, was constructed by Father Peter O'Farrell in the 1930s. The railings and water font came originally from the Chapel of the Workhouse. The attractive shrubs and trees surrounding the grotto were donated by parishioners.

Lourdes Grotto. *Photo: Sr. Maeve Brady.*

The "Iron" Church

Constructed of iron – this church was built in the townland of Tubber in 1861. It was blown down in the year 1904. the windows and gate were installed at R. Stephenson's home in Cloughernal, Granard.

The "Iron" Church. *Photo: R.W. Stafford.*

Photo: R.W. Stafford.

Masonic Hall

This Hall on the Ballinalee Road was built in 1893, destroyed by fire in 1917, and re-erected in 1919. The emblem on the front of the building represents two of the mason's tools of trade.

Masonic Hall – Exterior. *Photo: Ian White.*

Masonic Hall – Interior. *Photo: Sr. Maeve Brady.*

St. Mary's Abbey

The foundation of this Cistercian Abbey is ascribed to Richard de Tuiite in the year 1205. The Cistercian tabulae give the year 1214. This could refer to the year in which the monastic buildings were completed. The foundation was made from St. Mary's Abbey, Dublin. The first Abbot whom we know was Nigellus, in 1231.

The scanty ruins of the Abbey give no idea of what it looked like in the 13th century. All Cistercian houses were built to a common plan. The buildings were constructed in the form of a quadrangle round an open space, the church being on the north side. Opening onto this central space were the cloisters which led to the other buildings – Chapter House, Parlour, Scriptorum, Refectory, Kitchen and Storerooms. The dormitory was entered by a small stairs, while another stairs, known as the night stairs, led directly into the church. Most of the winding stairs is still intact, as is also a "Sile na Gig" – a female exhibitionist figure, one of many representations of lust in Romanesque sculpture.

For more than a century this Abbey was an Anglo-Norman outpost and **figures in a Remonstrance (1317)** addressed to the Holy See by Irish **princes**. It alleged "that the monks of the Cistercian order of Abbeylara **make their appearance publicly in arms**".

The Abbey was raided and plundered by Edward Bruce on 30th November, 1315. The monks fled to Athlone, the Scots and their Irish **allies remained in the Abbey for the winter.** Before the end of the 14th century the monastery had come under the influence of the rulers of Annaly – the O'Farrell family.

St. Mary's Abbey, Abbeylara.

Photo: Sr. Maeve Brady.

In 1355 Domhnall Mac Seoin Ui Fhearghail, taoiseach, died and was buried in Abbeylara. In 1398 Murchadh Bán died and, according to the annals, was buried in the resting place of his father and grandfather.

In 1411 Richard Uí Fearghail, monk, was the first of a long line of Abbots chosen from the ruling family of Annaly.

According to a Papal Register, "The Monastery was materially in a bad state and parts of the building had collapsed on account of wars and other calamities, which had long afflicted these parts." In Roman Registers the monastery is invariably named the "Monastery of the Blessed Virgin at Granard".

The amount of lands claimed by the Monastery varied according to the abbots' temporal authority. At one period the land extended into five parishes and included Lickbla in Co. Westmeath, Clonmacnoise and half of Inch Island in Lough Gowna.

The following list includes some of the Abbots:—

Abbot Nigellus	(1231—);
Abbot William Payne	(1319—1340);
Abbot Philip Nangle	(1388—1396);
Abbot Richard O'Farrell (Monk)	(1397—1422);
Bishop Cornelius	(1418—1424);
Abbot James O'Farrell	(1454—1464);
William O'Farrell (Chieftain)	(1497—1516);
Richard O'Farrell (Bishop)	(1542—1553).

Some Abbots became Bishops of Ardagh while retaining the position of Abbot *in commendam.*

In 1540 Henry VII caused the dissolution of the Monastery and the confiscation of its lands. The last Abbot to rule the Abbey was Richard O'Farrell. Instead of the survey or extent of the Abbey being made before a jury at or near the site, the legal formalities were carried out at Tristenagh Abbey in the Moyvore/Ballynacargy area. The reason given, "because we did not venture to approach nearer for fear of the Irish".

During the reign of Philip and Mary the lands "were granted forever *in capite* to Richard Nugent, royalties excepted".

The Abbey was the burial ground for many of the O'Farrell chieftains; John O'Farrell (1383), Donal O'Farrell (1385), Murchada Ban O'Farrell (1475). Mulconroy, historian to the O'Farrells and a relative of one of the Four Masters, is reputed to be buried there. Other noted burials include O'Keenan, Ollamh of the Maguires of Fermanagh (1495); Father Fergus Lee (1745), and Father P. Kiernan (1785). A few local families still retain their right to be buried in the monastery grounds.

With the decline and eventual closure of the Monastery, Abbeylara lost **its importance while Granard continued** to gain prestige.

A Walk around Granard

1. Foundation stone of Workhouse.
2. Cartronwillan Lane, site of military barracks.
3. Greville Arms Hotel.
4. Market House.
5. Buttermarket.
6. Cornmarket.
7. Diarmuid & Grainne's Cave.
8. Fernmount House.
9. Mills Lane, old schoolhouse.
10. Lourdes Grotto.
11. Motte.
12. '98 Memorial and Confessional Stone.
13. Foundation Stone for Granard's 1st National School.
14. Moxham Street Methodist Church Window.
15. Water Lane.
16. Tuite's Lane.
17. Foundation Stone (1708) of shop.
18. Springlawn House.

Gate of Market House. *Photo: Ian White.*

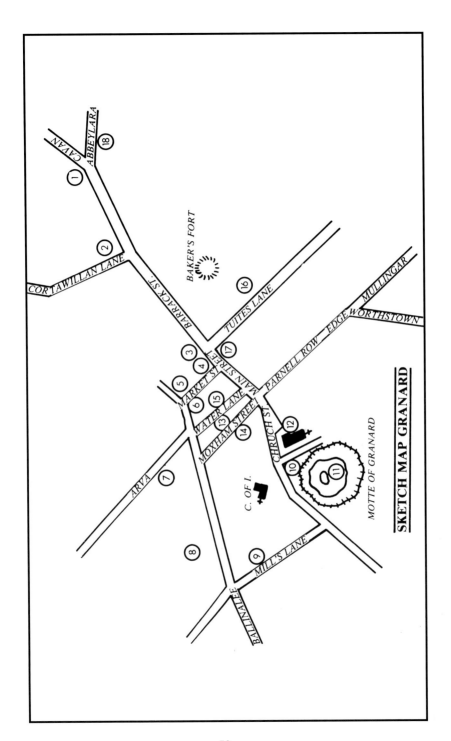

Schools

The monks had been the chief educators but when the monasteries were dissolved the Penal Laws effectively outlawed the education of Catholics. Education was imparted by the Hedge School Master who taught at the risk of his freedom.

The Relief Act of 1772 restored to Catholics the right to teach in schools and by the year 1826 Granard had nine schools — one Parish School and eight Pay Schools.

Pay Schools

The Master charged a rate of 1½d to 3d per pupil per week, so several schools existed in open competition with each other. The buildings varied in description from a "miserable hovel" to classes held in the upper floor of the Market House.

The Royal Commission set up in 1824 to enquire into the state of education in Ireland issued nine Reports. The Parochial Abstracts are given in Appendix No. 22 of the Reports. It should be noted that the Parochial boundaries are those of the Established Church.

Moxham Street School. *Photo: A. Burns.*

This school was erected by subscriptions in 1820, the Vicar being Rev. Christopher Robinson, the curate Rev. G. R. Robinson. The building, which included living accommodation for teachers, was of stone and slated. Fees were charged but free education was given to the poor as the school was supported by the Board of Erasmus Smyth and the Kildare Place Society. H. James and Sarah Mills taught here, hence the name 'Mills Lane". Bronterre O'Brien was a pupil. The school closed in 1963.

School – Mills' Lane. *Photo: R.W. Staffprd.*

In 1831, the Stanley Act set up a system of primary education in National Schools. In 1834 a National School for Boys was built in Moxham Street. There were 167 boys and one teacher, whose yearly salary was £12.

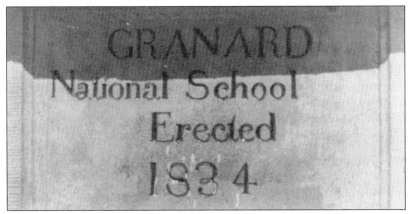

Photo: R.W. Stafford.

A Girls' School was build in Cartronwillan Lane. In 1849 there were 89 girls enrolled and one teacher, whose yearly salary was £8.

In 1842 the Workhouse was established complete with schools. The records for 1850 show that there were 269 males and 417 females enrolled – a total of 686 pupils, one male teacher and one female teacher. No mention is made re salary.

In 1871 the 'Classical School of Granard', known as St. Bernard's, was founded. It was held in the upper floor of Moxham Street School. It continued for 24 years. The principal teachers were Rev. M. Gilligan (1871 - 1876), Rev. John H. Galligan (1882 - 1895) and Canon Patrick Dolan (1882 - 1895). *(See Personalities).*

The building for many years was known as 'The Band School', as it was used as a practice room for the Granard Brass and Reed Band and the Accordian Band. In later years it was called Moxham Street Hall, and served as a meeting place for many parish organisations until its demolition in 1986.

Springlawn House. *Photo: Ian White.*

The Presentation Sisters

The history of education in Granard is interwoven with the history of the Religious Sisters who came to live in the town.

On 12th october, 1871, six sisters left the Presentation Convent in George's Hill, Dublin to travel by train to Granard. They were met by the Bishop, Rev. Dr. Conroy and Fr. McGaver, P.P. They were given accommodation by the Pettit family at Springlawn House.

On 21st November — Presentation Day — their "Pension" School for girls was opened. The names of the sisters were — Sr. Brigid Reynolds (died 1906), Sr. Joseph Kealing (died 1906), Sr. Frances Moore (died 1907), Mother Emeria Harbinson (died 1908) Sr. Margaret Atkinson (died 1909) and Sr. M. Teresa Miliffe (died 1922).

The Presentation Sisters at that time were a semi enclosed order so the arrangements in Granard were not suitable for their requirements. In 1882 the six sisters departed for Portadown, Co. Armagh. A plaque, recording the gratitude of the townspeople to the Sisters, was erected in St. Mary's Church.

Sisters of Mercy

Photo: Courtesy of the National Library of Ireland.

The Sisters of Mercy came from Newtownforbes Convent to Granard on 2nd February, 1881, their convent being at Springlawn. Three Sisters nursed in the Workhouse Infirmary – Sr. Mary of Mercy Flood, Sr. M. Francis Hoare and Sr. Magdalen Frost. Three other Sisters taught in the Workhouse School – Sr. Gertrude Quinlan, Sr. Bernard McGuire and Sr. Brigid Burke. Two Sisters – Sr. Michael Glancy and Sr. Stanislaus also taught in a school in what are now outhouses at Springlawn House.

The Sisters were very poor but were supported by the kindness and generosity of the people of Granard, some of whom were not co-religionists. They lived for 13 years in Springlawn. The present Convent was built in 1892 – 94 in the monastic style of the period. Extensions were later added, maintaining the original style.

This Bronze Bell was used in the Workhouse and later erected on the primary school cloister. When the present school was built the bell was removed but its life was not over! A Holy Ghost Father brought the bell back to his mission church in Africa.

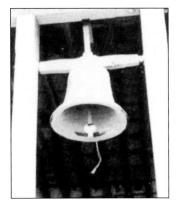

Photo: Sr. Carmel O'Reilly.

Girls' National School 1891. *Photo: Sisters of Mercy.*

In 1891 the Sisters of Mercy were chiefly responsible for having a new Girls National School erected. This school served the needs of the town until it too was replaced in 1977 by Scoil an Chroí Naofa.

Scoil an Chroí Naofa. *Photo: Aidan Corcoran.*

Principals of Sacred Heart National School:–
Sister Rose McSharry
Sister Dolores Finnegan
Sister Eucharia O'Dwyer
Sister Ignatius Lucas
Sister Nancy Clarke
Sister Carmel O'Reilly

The Class of '46/47

Third row: Patricia Harton, Rose Smyth, Anne Cullen, Maureen Cosgrove, Catherine Fagan, Mairead Gaffney, Margaret Donaghue.
Second row: Betty Mulligan, Jane Columb, Kitty Daly, Maureen Daly, Nellie Tynan, Sheila Coyle, Rose Reilly, Noelle Burns.
Front row: Mary Donnelly, Brigid Keegan, Maureen Cullen, Dympna Cullen, Cáit Dale, Patricia Gaffney, Anne Masterson, Amelia Meehan, Ita Meehan, Kathleen Clyne.

Photo: R. Sheridan.

School Drama - 1955

Back row: Mai Lynch, Monica Murray, Amelia Meehan, Moll Lynch, Mairead Walsh, Sadie Tynan, Betty Kenny, Cait Dale, Maeve Barry, Margaret Fitzgerald, Bridgie Cullen, Maureen Daly, Doris Geraghty, Margot Kiernan, Teresa Brady, Rosie Smyth.

Photo: R. Sheridan.

PARISH OF GRANA[RD]

Name of Townland or Place at which the School is held	Name of Master or Mistress	Religion of Master or Mistress	Free or Pay School	Total Annual In[come] of Master or Mi[stress] Arising in all [ways] from the Sch[ool]
Killina	Thomas Fegan	R. Catholic	Pay	from £6 to £[ ]
Muckerstaff	Michael Flood	R. Catholic	Pay	£10
Tully	William Murtagh	R. Catholic	Pay	£12
Leitrim	John Mulvanny	R. Catholic	Pay	£9
Ramogue	Thomas McGorrell	R. Catholic	Pay	about £10
Bonlahy	Edward Hughes	R. Catholic	Pay	£7
Granard	Owen Lynch	R. Catholic	Pay	£30
Granard	Rose Fitzpatrick	R. Catholic	Pay	£7
Granard	Farrell Gilchrist	R. Catholic	Pay	£25
Granard	Michael McGoughan	R. Catholic	Pay	£18
Granard	Anthony Sheridan	R. Catholic	Pay	£50
Granard	Charles Carolan	R. Catholic	Pay	£35
Aughnagarron	Patrick Flood	R. Catholic	Pay	from £15 to £1[ ]
Granard	James Mills and Sara Mills	Protestants	Free and Pay	£37
Granard	John McGee	R. Catholic	Pay	£18
Granard	Ellenor Geoghegan	R. Catholic	Pay	from 2d. to 4d. p.[w] for each schola[r]
Springtown	John Donoghue	R. Catholic	Pay	about £8
Cloughurnel	Hugh McKernan	R. Catholic	Pay	£8. 10s.
Dalystown	Patrick Monaghan	R. Catholic	Pay	£9. 2s.
Ballysunna	James Byrne	R. Catholic	Pay	1½d. per week fr[ee] scholar
Ballymorice	Thady McNaly	R. Catholic	Pay	£8
Magheraly	Mrs. Anne O'Neill	R. Catholic	Pay	1½d. per week fr[om] each scholar

AROCHIAL ABSTRACTS 1826

scription of the hoolhouse and able cost thereof	Number of Pupils in Attendance on an Average of Three Months Preceding this Return By the Roman Catholic Return			Societies, Associations, etc. with which the School is connected, or whether assisted by local patronage and in what manner, stating such as Parish Schools	Scriptures whether Read or Not in the School
	Protestants				
	Established Church	Presby- terians	Roman Catholics		
st miserable hovel.	—	—	36	none	not read
walls, thatched; £5.	6	—	40	none	read; A.V.
d house, intended a barn.	17	4	23	none	not stated
& clay, thatched; ed at £2 per annum.	5	—	45	none	read; A.V. 1 copy
y bad room.	—	—	49	none	not stated
m in a hired cabin	3	—	46	none	not read
ted house; rented 5 per annum.	3	—	46	none	read; A.V.
d hovel; rented at per annum	—	—	33	none	not stated
and clay; rented £2 16s. 8d. per um	—	—	90	none	not read
thatched house; ed at £2 per um	2	—	48	none	read; A.V. 1 copy
d house; rented at per annum	1	—	25	none	read; in Greek
upper part of the rket house	5	—	9	none	read; in Greek
ched house, used as ster's dwelling; t £7	1	—	70	none	not read
d slated house with partments for the ster	46	3	31	The Parish School The Board of Erasmus Smith and the Kildare Place Society. The Master receives £7 from a charge on a neighbouring parish. Schoolhouse built partly by subscriptions	read; A.V.
by subscription d by grant of £50 n the Association for ountenancing Vice					
apartment in the ster's dwellinghouse; ed at £12 per annum	—	—	24	none	not read
upper room in a ging house	—	—	14	none	not read
retched hovel	2	—	35	none	read; V. n.s. 1 copy
oor mud wall hovel	—	—	36	none	not read
iserable hut, built r a cow house; cost	—	—	' 70	none	not stated
nall thatched cabin; nted at 10d. per week	5	—	55	none	not stated
iserable hovel, in nich a cow is fed	—	—	40	none	not stated
ud wall cabin	15	—	10	none	not stated

Cnoc Mhuire

In 1947 the Secondary School was opened in the Workhouse Lodge. Twenty-four pupils were enrolled. Each year the number of pupils increased. In 1954 Cnoc Mhuire became Ireland's second co-educational Secondary School to be staffed by nuns. In 1970 and 1982 the buildings were extended to provide even better facilities for the growing number of pupils.

Cnoc Mhuire, Granard. *Photo: Aiden Corcoran.*

In 1930 the Vocational Educational Act was passed and for some time classes were held in the Workhouse buildings. In 1949 the classes moved to the Town Hall. 1953 saw the establishment of the present Vocational School and the fact that it had to be extended in 1969 and 1982 is proof of its continuing success.

Granard Vocational School. *Photo: R.W. Stafford.*

Boys' School

Photo: Ian White.

A National School for Boys was built "on the hill" in 1891. It is the only school in the parish which had a teacher's residence.

Teacher's Residence. *Photo: Ian White.*

The teachers who lived in the residence were Master Pat Reilly, Masters Cosgrave, McNiffe, Farrell, Reid, McGrath and Fitzgibbon.

1st row bottom, l. to r.: J. burns, J. Cunningham, P. Daly, Andy Brown, Ned Kelly, P. Hourican, J. Gerty, J. Hynes, F. Rock, E. Hourican. 2nd row, l. to r.: J. Coyle, C. O'Shea, James Kellet, B. Finnan, P. Conlon, J. Murphy, P. McGovern, O. Brien, W. Hyland, B. Sheddock. 3rd row, l. to r.: M. Murphy, T. Brown, Ned Lynn, L. O'Brien, T. Sheridan, O'Brien, B. Murphy, M. Kelly, R. Nugent, J. Kelly, T. Corcoran. Back row, l. to r.: C. Brogan, J.J. Kelly, P. McGovern, Joseph Gerty, H. Devine, J. Murphy (Gandi), Ned Kelly, Rory McCabe, Matt Coyle, P. Cuffe. Teacher: P. Griffin (3rd row).

Photo: T. Kiernan.

St. Mary's Boys National School — 1961

Back row: Leo Kelly, R.I.P., Seamus Smyth, John Regan, P.J. Dunne, Paddy Kilbride, Thomas Devine, Martin Sheridan, Raymond Dunne, Tommy Kelly, Des Cummins, Francis Campbell, Hugh Flynn and Noel Monahan. *Photo: Mrs. E. Regan.*

Mills Lane School — Class c.1930

Anna Bogan, Miss Blennerhassett (teacher), Dolly Moore, George Cox, David Cox, Maud Flemming, Jim Baird, Harry Grier, Lettie Gilpin, Richard Gilpin, Cecil Moore, Norman Furlong, Alfred Francis, Eileen Moore.

Country Schools

Killasonna School
Photo: Ian White.

Built in 1892, this replaced a small school in the townland of Aughabrack, about a quarter of a mile north of Killasonna crossroads.
  There have been only three principals in the school –
Peter Higgins – 1894-1933   Mrs. Mary Gavigan – 1933-1955   Mrs. R. Kennedy – 1955-

Bunlahy School
Photo: Ian White.

This school was built in 1885 by Archdeacon O'Flanagan P.P.V.G. The school is dedicated to St. Gusacht, the first Bishop of Granard.
  Principals –

Mr. Cassidy or Mr. Sammon		John MacDevitt	—	1944-1948
Bernard Brady	— 1900-1928	John Carthy	—	1948-1951
Patrick Trapp		Joe McKelvey	—	1951-1965
Joseph Timoney	— 1929-1930	Sylvester Hyland	—	1965-1967
John O Sé	— 1930-1943	C. Boyle	—	1967-
Nicholas Kearney	— 1943-1944			

Killeen School

In 1840 there was a boys and girls school in Killeen. This was replaced by the 'old' school in 1890 (see photo). The most recent building (St. Patrick's School) was opened in 1965.

Photo: Ian White.

Principals of the school since 1928:–
Mr. P. Greene, who still lives in Ballinalee, taught prior to 1928.
Mr. Duignan   1928-1957   Mr. David Lowery   1959-1971
Mr. M. Fitzgibbon   1957-1959   Mr. Brendan O'Beirne 1971-

St. Patrick's School.   *Photo: Ian White.*

People of Granard

Grevilles

The Greville family of Clonhugh, Mullingar had long associations with the Granard area. In the 1820s they purchased their property in the northern section of Granard from the Forbes family. Patrick, Lord Greville represented Longford in Westminster from 1852–1869. He gave Barrack Street to Rev. Burrows.

In 1893 Granard Urban Council purchased more of the Greville property which considerably decreased his holding in the area.

The last surviving member of the family was Miss Carmelita Greville who died in Paris in the 1940s.

The name lives on in the townland of Greville and the still flourishing Greville Arms Hotel in the town.

John Dungan
Born in Granard in 1730. He emigrated to Copenhagen and became a ship merchant by the year 1780. He took a great interest in music and regretted the decline of the Irish harp. To encourage harpists he sent "at least twenty-three guineas" as prize money for a competition at the first Ball to be held in Granard in 1781. He came back to Granard in 1785 for the third Ball and spent some time in the area. He returned to Copenhagen where he died on the 8th February, 1804.

Michael Gaffney
Born in Cartron, Granard, in 1775. He emigrated to America in 1797 where he became wealthy and well known. He founded a town called Gaffney in 1808 in which there is a Granard Street. He was a Captain in the militia in the resumed Revolutionary War of 1812 - 1814 and took the side of the U.S.A. He died in 1854 and a monument was erected to his memory in the Main Street of Gaffney.

James Bronterre O'Brien
Born in Granard in 1804, eldest child of Daniel and Mary (nee Kearney). His ancestors came from Rincoola where some of his mother's relatives still live. He emigrated to England in 1829 where he later founded the Chartist Movement. He published "Bronterre's First Letter to the People of England" in 1831. He died in 1864 and was buried in Abbey Park Cemetery. His biography entitled "Bronterre" was written by Alfred Plummer.

Bronterre O'Brien aged 46.
From a daguerreotype
photograph taken in 1850.

Rev. Thomas Mills – Hymnologist
Born near Granard in 1825 he graduated from Trinity College in 1852 and was appointed Rector of St. Jude's, Dublin, where he remained for 43 years. He was a composer of Hymns and Songs and contributed to "The Nation". He died in Dublin in 1900. A memorial window was erected in St. Jude's.

Canon P. Dolan

Born Upper Main Street Granard about 1860. He was on the staff of St. Mel's College in 1882. From 1883 to 1896 he was Curate in Granard and taught in St. Bernard's Classical School, which was held in the upper storey of Moxham Street Hall. In 1897 he was appointed Administrator and Chaplain to the Workhouse in Longford. In 1903 he became Parish Priest of Aughavas and in 1920 he was transferred to Bornacoola and subsequently named a Canon. He inherited the estate of his brother Dr. Dolan, and set up a trust to provide food and clothing for the needy children of Granard. He died on the 3rd January 1933.

Patrick Dunleavy

Born in Granard in 1891. He emigrated to America and became a horticulturist and poet. He died in 1957. His son, J. P. Donleavy, born in America but now living at Levington Park, near Mullingar, is a well known author.

Thomas Kilbride

Thomas Kilbride, Cartron, Granard, was a long serving member of Longford County Council and Granard Town Commissioners being chairman of both bodies on several occasions. He was also a member of County Longford Committee of Agriculture and the Midland Health Board, and chairman of County Longford Executive Fine Gael.

He was elected to the Senate on the Agricultural Panel from 1973 – 1982. He died in September 1986.

Tommy Kilbride.

Dr. Brian Cusack
Son of Mr. and Mrs. Andrew Cusack, Main Street, Granard (now Durkin's shop): T.D. for Galway in first Dáil.

DÁIL ÉIREANN, AN TARNA TIONOL, 10 ABRAN, 1919 — Sreath 1 – (i dtosach): L. MacFhionnghail, M. O'Coileain, C. Brugha, A. O'Griobhtha, E. de Bhailera, S. Conte Pluingcéad, E. MacNéill, L. MacCosgair, E. de Blaghd. Sreath 2 – P. O'Maodhomhnaigh, T. MacSuibhne, R. O'Maolchatha, S. O'Dochartaigh, S. O'Mathghamhna, S. O'Deolain, S. MacAonghusa, P. O'Caoimh, M. MacStain, S. MacCraith, An Dr. B. O'Ciosog, L. de Roiste, L. Colibhet, An tA. M. O'Flannagain. Sreath 3 – P. Mac an Bhaird, A. MacCaba, D. MacGearailt, S. MacSuibhne, An Dr. R. O hAodha, C. O'Coileain, P. O'Maille, S. O'Meadhra, B. O hUigin, S. de Burca, S. O hUigin. Sreath 4 – S. MacDonnchadha, S. Mac an tSaoi. Sreath 5 – P. Beaslaoi, R. Bartuin, P. O'Callagain. Sreath 6 – P. O'Seanachain, S. Etchingham.   *Photo: L. Kiernan.*

Kitty Kiernan

Kitty Kiernan, the fiancée of Michael Collins, was born in Granard in 1892. She was educated at Loreto Convent, Bray, and later at St. Ita's, the school founded in Dublin by Padraig Pearse. Kitty was one of four sisters who lived with their brother Larry, the proprietor of the Greville Arms Hotel. The sisters supervised the running of the Hotel and the adjoining grocery, bar and hardware store.

Kitty first met Michael Collins in May 1917 when he stayed at the Hotel with his friend and fellow worker Harry Boland during a by-election campaign in Longford. Both men were smitten by the charming and vivacious Kitty, but it was to Collins that she gave her heart. They kept up a lengthy correspondence when Collins returned to Dublin. Even through the delicate Treaty negotiations in London he wrote to her every day. These letters are the subject of a recently published book by Leon O Broin under the title *In Great Haste.*

Throughout those difficult years Kitty suffered great worry and anxiety regarding Collins' wellbeing and her worst fears were realised when her "Laughing Boy" was assassinated at Béal na Bláth on 22nd August 1922.

She married Felix Cronin, Quartermaster General of the National Army, in 1925. She died in 1945 and is buried in Glasnevin cemetery, not far from where Collins lies.

DEDICATED TO
Miss Kitty Kiernan.

A MESSAGE

SONG

WORDS BY
L. CADIZ.

MUSIC BY
DERMOT MACMURROUGH

PRICE 2/- NET.

A MESSAGE.

I plucked a pale proud lily
  That lone in a garden grew,
I thought it would bear a message
  Of the love in my heart for you.

Wet on the face of the lily
  Like tears the dewdrops lay,
Did it presage to me the sorrow
  That would come to me some day.

For I laid that lovely lily
  On your cold still breast, dear love,
And the tears in my heart are buried
  Till we'll meet in God's home above.

Kitty Kiernan. *Photo: L. Kiernan.*

Eddie Macken

Eddie Macken, born and reared in Main Street, Granard, is considered to be one of the greatest showjumpers in the world. His enthusiasm for horses showed at an early age when he successfully competed at local shows and competitions on "Granard Boy". His talents have won him championships in Europe, Canada, U.S.A. and Australia. He has represented Ireland on the winning team for the Aga Khan Trophy on many occasions. On "Boomerang" Eddie set an unprecedented record by winning the Hickstead Derby in England in 1976, 1977, 1978 and 1979. Eddie received due recognition for his achievements when he featured on the I.T.V. Programme *This is Your Life.*

Eddie Macken.

Brendan O'Reilly

Brendan O'Reilly, well-known Reporter, Presenter and T.V. Host with R.T.É., was born and spent nine years of his childhood in Granard.

He achieved athletic fame as an Irish and British high jump champion, Irish javelin and decathlon record holder and was selected to the 1956 Irish Olympic team.

Brendan is also a successful songwriter/composer and poet. He composed the new International Olympic song *Let the Nations Play* and topped the charts with his *Ballad of Michael Collins*.

He has achieved fame both on stage and in films.

Brendan O'Reilly.

Larry Cunningham.

Larry Cunningham

Larry Cunningham, born near Granard, is a household name on the music scene both at home and abroad. He performs every year at the Folk Festival in Nashville, Tennessee. Specialising in Country and Folk music, he has played and broadcast throughout Europe and America.

Traces of Irish in everyday use
in the Granard area

Gahellas: *Girls*
Gosoons: *Boys*
Amac/Sonsín amac:
   To address a young boy
Amadán: *Foolish person*
Gallaces: *Braces*
Geansaí: *Jumper*
Clownies: *Marriage relations*
Sleeveen: *Sly person*
Gob: *Mouth*
Pus: *Angry face*
Spág: *Big foot*
Clábar: *Muck*
Glár: *Muck*
Scrád: *Sod*
Traithnín: *Blade of grass*
Traithnin treseach: *Hoar-frost*
Buachalán: *Ragwort*
Bootrie: *Elder tree*
Kesh: *Colvert, bridge*
Loig: *Tool for digging*
Scolb: *Stick for thatching*
Pratties: *Potatoes*
Stibhin: *Stick for planting potatoes*
Praiscín: *Seedbag for potatoes*
Poirín: *Small potatoes*
Banbh: *Young pig*
Ceiseog: *Young sow*

Puc: *Hit*
Blas: *Accent*
Flathuile: *Generous*
Whist: *Be quiet!*
Cogaring: *Whispering*
A lock: *A small amount*
Go leor: *Enough*
Lan a' mhála: *Enough*
Trake: *Germ*
Haskie: *East wind weather*
Drawkie. *Damp weather*
Kippeens. *Small sticks*
Greesheach: *Embers*
Clamp: *Stack*
Scaldeen: *Fledgling*
Cludóg: *Children's Easter Feast of boiled hen eggs*
Mantóg: *Silly*
Gobán. *Used on a calf's mouth*
Panakeen: *Tin mug.*
Tá an Teach A Thógaill: *The house is a' building (direct translation)*
Tre Sleamhan: *Field in townland of Clough, where the three parishes of Abbeylara, Colmcille and Granard meet.*
Griskeens: *Pork fillets*
Gonc: *Disappointment*

Family Names

Some of the following list of surnames of families now living in the Granard area, date back to the 17th century. Those marked ** are named in the 1657 Census, the rest date from the 1837 Census.

Bennet	**Duffy	Keegan	**Mahon	**Sheridan
Bogan	**Donoghue	**Kelly	Major	Slevin
**Brady	Early	Kenny	**Mulligan	**Smith
Brown	Fagan	King	**Masterson	Smyth
Burns	**Farrell	**Kiernan	Monahan	Stephenson
Coyle	**Flood	Kilbride	**Nugent	Tynan
Clarke	Gilpin	Lee	**O'Hara	Walsh
Cunningham	Grier	Lynch	Pettit	
Corcoran	Gilligan	**McCabe	Quinn	
**Connell	Heany	**Maguire	**Reilly	
Daly	Higgins	**McHugh	Small	

Art Ó Ceallaigh

(1)
Bí mé lá fada ag dul trasna na tíre
'S buaileadh go teach Airt Uí Cheallaigh san oíche mé
Mar a bhfuair mé teach folamh gan duine ná daoine
Agus shuidh mé ag an teine ag léigheamh mo sgéiste

(2)
Tainic Art isteach chugam ar buile 's ar daoire
Is oiread bréid salainn in' agall dá innaois leis
"What in the divil, a dhuine tá mbínn tú
Nó cad €an cat mara do chas i mo tír tú

(3)
Is annamh sin traveller ag teacht chun mo thíghe-se
Ní tainic ariamh agus ní tiocfaidh go deó
Cá bíonn sa anseo 'noir' ach mise 'm'inghean beag
Agus dá marbhadh mátair nach bhfuil neam dó didean

(4)
Muise is mairg don athair a shíol tú
Cá dtiubhraí sin dósan fosgadh ná dídean
Míle glóir d'Dia nach bhfuil a dhath de mo ghaol leat
Mar duine tú, Airt ghrobhuig nach cosmhail le Críost-éide"

(5)
Sguir de do sheanmhóir is stad de do shiamsa
Cad chuige nach luigh tú le cois claidhe na dighe
Ní dul chun tíghe tabhairne ag eagal do pighinn ann
Trath binnse 'mo threablóir is mar sin do ghnídhim

(6)
Bí níor aitheas teach tabhairne rómham sa tslighe seo
Mur racham go Granard fán taca so d'oíche
Is tá siad ina gcodladh 'sba doiligh leo éirghe
Is níorbh fhiú dí dólaid mé an tasdar a dhéanamh

(7)
Níl an teach tabhairne comh fada agus silir
Tá an oíche ag cur sneachta 's an ghealach ag éirghe
Siúd suas an bealach is lean é go díreach
Go Droichead na Caileach 'sgo Carcumnag Caomhtheach

(8)
"Cá dtéighim-se amach comh bog réidh is shin
Tá ró-mhór é m'parteios go gcaspaide an sluagh síde dom
Ní raibh leithéide again ann is ní bíonn a choíche
Ach is próingí créideas an rinne darb díot tú"

(9)
[Thaith chum ar Art mé cur amach le n'a chríonnacht
Dhúisigh sé is ghabh sé leat sgéal ba saoitheamhail
'Is cosmhail nár léig tú Scripture ná bíobla
Ach dá marbhadh athair inariphad se leog duit]

(10)
Níl a fhios agam nach spealfin ón Mide tú
A ghoidfeadh mo hata mo báta 'smo brísde
A ghoidfeadh an casur beag i bpraetait an tíghe agam
An crom-cum coimhil 'smo iurad beag píopa".

(11)
Chuaidh Art a chodladh gan corraigh an oíche sin
Ar chuntar an aitis nach dtainig sé éirghe
D'fhágh sé mise sa gcúdhionaigh mhaomig
Mo shuídh ar an leaba 'so m'gean ar taoibh dhíom

(12)
Labhair an ógbhean de comhrád caoitheamhail
"tiofaidh do chiall agat nóin maiream do caomheach
Nó dá mbead fios agam gur duine dim ghaol tú
Coimhreochann do leaba dhuit agus cuirfinn do luighe tú"

(13)
Chuir mé lámh uimpi, a inisle mo chroídhe tú!
Más inghean d'Art tú tá tú léghach saoitheamhail
Is mór é mo ghean ort, a chailín ghroideamhail,
Go deimhin féin caithfinn leat cathamhas míosa

Art Ó Ceallaigh was composed by Peter Connell, Cranary, Granard. Arthur O'Neill, the blind harpist, said "that Peter could sing well and compose well." It is a fine example of Irish as spoken in the Granard area.

Lakes, Rivers and Wells
The Lure of Blue Water

Few towns in Ireland can compare with Granard's wealth of angling waters. Strategically placed between two major rivers — the Shannon and Erne — it is within easy reach of both of them and has its own 'lake district'.

Ballinlough and **Killeen** lakes, in townlands of the same names, are good waters for pike and roach and can be fished from boat or shore.

Lough na Gower (Lake of the goats) lies between the townlands of Ballymaurice and Cartron and has yet to be developed. The 'sister lakes' of **Kinale, Derragh** and **Bracklagh** have a plentiful supply of coarse fish.

Lough Sheelin (the fairy lake) has been restocked in recent years and is considered to be one of Ireland's greatest lakes for trout. It is a favourite haunt for anglers both from home and abroad.

Lough Mullinroe is a very good pike water but access to the lake needs to be developed.

Lough Gowna is a well known coarse fishing centre. It is also a very picturesque lake surrounded by low hills and wooded shoreland and has many islands. The river Erne has its source here.

The Spout.   *Photo: Sr. Maeve Brady.*

The Spout

The Spout is an old Granard landmark with an unfailing supply of spring water. Before the coming of piped water there were street pumps in Barrack Street and at the Diamond, also a well in Water Lane. In 1952 a pumphouse was built at Lough Kinale and Granard got its piped water supply.

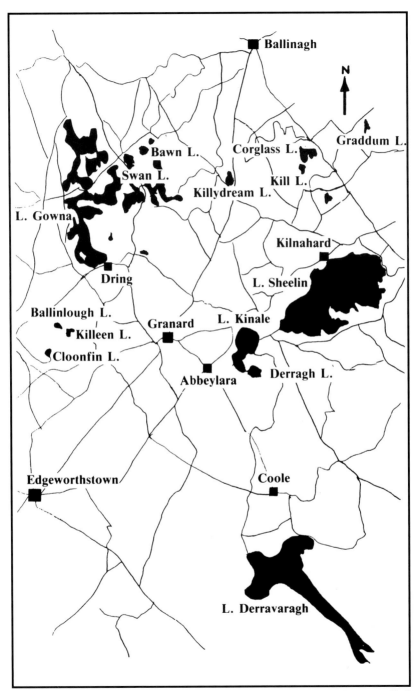

Granard's Lakeland. *Skeetch: R.W. Stafford.*

Rivers

Ballinlough River runs from Killeen Lough to Ballinlough.

Curbawn River (Cor Ban, white round hill) flows from the west end of Ballinlough through Clonfin Lough and thence into the parish of Clonbroney.

River Rhine – runs in a north-westerly direction and falls into the eastern end of Killeen Lough.

Camlin River – the water from several small streams and springs in the area eventually converge to form the Camlin near "Droichead na gCailleach" at Ferriskill. It meanders to Longford town en route to the Shannon at Clondra.

The **River Inny** which flows from the eastern shore of Lough Kinale is excellent water for pike, perch, roach and tench.

Holy Wells

Tobar-na-mban naomh: Well of the Saintesses or Holy Women, is situated in the village of Abbeylara, on the right-hand side of a small pass off the main road from Granard to the graveyard. (Ref.: Fr. McGivney – *Placenames of Longford*).

Tobar Gamhna: Well of the Calf. In the townland of Rathbracken this curious and ancient well is said to be the fountain spring of the great Lough Gowna.

Tobar Righ an Domhnaigh: Tobereendoney. This well is situated in the townland of Ballyboy near the stream which forms the border with Rincoola. When O'Donovan visited the area in 1837, he recorded that it "was a very sacred fountain", and that "man only can taste its waters with impunity" and recounts strange happenings. *(See Folklore section.)*

St. Patrick's Well, Cartron. St. Patrick found Cairbre's druids performing their superstitious rites here. He blessed it and allowed the natives to continue their veneration but directed their worship to Jesus. (Ref. Journal of Ardagh & Clonmacnoise Antiquarian Society, 1940.) Pilgrims still visit the well leaving tokens on an adjacent bush. The well is most easily reached by a stile on Edgeworthstown Road near the Spout – (surplus water from the well). It is situated in the third field in a north-west direction in the townland of Cartron.

Flora and Fauna

North County Longford, including the Granard area, has some interesting botanical features, many of which have only been discovered in recent years by amateur botanists.

The main features include forest and lakelands; also many old undeveloped meadows. This type of plant habitat is fast disappearing as lime spreading, drainage and reseeding of so called marginal land increases. There are also tracts of waste ground, areas with impervious soils, riverside meadows, cut-away bog and odd corners of otherwise productive fields all of which hold considerable botanical interest.

Lesser Celandine. *Photo: Sean Howard.*

Derrycassan Wood has a great variety of plant life even though it is mainly coniferous forest.

Lough Kinale has most of the species of plant life found around other midland lakes.

The Ballywillan area where the disused railway exists is also a good source of plant life.

Plants growing in the Granard area which are rare or absent from the midlands include:—

(a) *Gallium mollugo* (Bedstraw) grows on the Motte.
(b) *Sedum reflexum* (Stonecrop) grows in abundance on walls near the Motte. This plant naturalises quite often.
(c) *Lepidum Heterophyllum* (Smith's Cress) grows in many locations around Granard, considered rare except in the South and East.
(d) *Salix repens* (Creeping Willow) is found growing in wet places in the area, this species is rare to the midlands.
(e) *Sisymbrium officinale* (Hedge Mustard) is found in the area, not recorded in central Ireland.
(f) *Nardus stricta* (Mat Grass) grows on Lough Gowna shore.
(g) *Viola tricolor* (Wild Pansy) grows freely in an old sand pit in Derrycassan Wood. This plant only occurs occasionally in the North and East.

(h) *Reynoutria japonica* a popular shrub in the last century with white flowers is growing wild in many neglected gardens around Granard.
(i) *Symphoricarpos rivularis* (Snowberry) – this shrub, also a garden escape, is abundant in Derragh, Abbeylara.
(j) *Dactylorhiza kerryensis* (Irish Marsh Orchid) grows by Lough Gowna, Lough Kinale near Ballywillan, Gallid and on Corn Hill.
(k) *Vinca minor* (Periwinkle) – a creeping shrub with blue flowers and waxy leaves grows abundantly by the stream in Derrycassan Wood. It probably has survived since cultivation as a garden species.
(l) *Harebell* grows in the Gallid area.

More common wild flowers and plants seen in the area are fragrant Orchids, Ragged Robin, Cornflowers, Vetch, Honeysuckle, Gorse and Broom.

The Granard area abounds in bird and animal life.

There is an active Gun Club, the members of which are not only involved in the sporting aspect, but in the preservation of fast-disappearing species of wild life and the control of vermin.

The most common animals include:- foxes, hares, badgers, grey squirrels, mink, hedgehogs, pinemarten and stoats. The grey squirrel was introduced to Ireland at Castleforbes, Co. Longford in 1911.

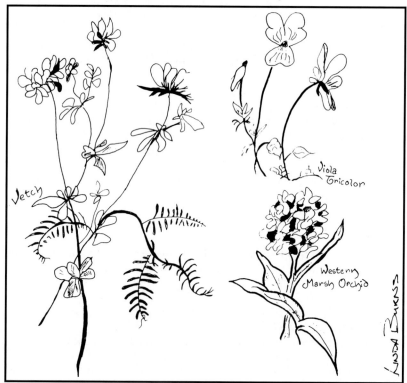

Birds

Varieties of **wild duck** to be seen in the area include:— Mallard, Pintail, Gadwall, Wigeon, Shoveller, Teal, Scaup, Tufted Duck and Red-crested Pochard.

Other River and Water Birds include:— Great-crested Grebe, Grey Heron, Swans, Greenland White-fronted Geese, Brent Geese, Moorhens, Coot, Curlews, Snipe, Plover and Lapwing.

Game Birds include:— Pheasant, Grouse (very rare), Quail (bob-white), which have recently been introduced, Pigeon, Doves, Cuckoo, Kingfisher, Barn Owls and Short-eared Owls.

Birds of Prey:— Kestrel, Sparrow Hawk, Raven, Magpie and Herring Gulls.

Townlands

1. **RATHBRACKEN**: *Rath Breacain* — Speckled fort.
2. **TOBER**: *Tobar* — a well.
3. **COOLCOR**: *Cúlcor* — Round back.
4. **CARTRONMARKEY**: *Cartrum a'mharcaigh* — Cartron of the horseman.
5. **KILLEEN**: *Coillín* — Little wood.
6. **BALLYMORE**: *Baile mór* — Large town.
7. **RATHCOR**: *Rath Chorr* — Odd fort.
8. **BALLYGILCHRIST**: *Baile mhic giolla chriost* — Gilchrist's town.
9. **GALLID**: *Gallaid* — a standing stone, pillar-stone.
10. **BALLYNAGALL**: *Baile na nGall* — Town of the foreigners.
11. **MULLANGEE**: *Muilleann gaoithe* — a windmill.
12. **CHURCHQUARTER**: *Ceathramhadh an Teampuill*.
13. **GRANARDKILLE**: *Granárd cille* — Church of the hill of the sun.
14. **BALLYBRIEN**: *Baile Úi Bhriain* — O'Brien's town.
15. **MOATFIELD**:

16. **GRANARD**: *Granárd* — Hill of the sun.
17. **GRASSLAND (YARD)**.
18. **RATHCRONAN**: *Rath Crónain* — Cronan's fort.
19. **TEEMORE**: *Tigh mór* — Large house.
20. **CARTRON**: *Cartrim* — A quarter portion of land.
21. **HIGGINSTOWN**: *Tochar na móna* — Causeway of the bog.
22. **BALLYMAURICE**: *Baile Muirghis* — People named Morris lived

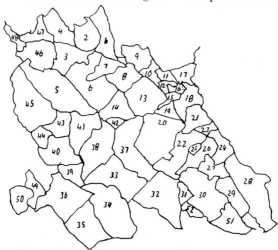

Townlands of Granard Parish.   *Sketch: Conor Murphy.*

23. **TEENYPHOBBLE**: *Teine phobail* — Fire of the tribe.
24. **ROBINSTOWN**.
25. **GREVILLE**.
26. **AGHABRACK**: *Acadh Breac* — Speckled field.
27. **TONEEN**: *Tuinín* — Little bottom land.
28. **RINCOOLAGH**: *Rinn chulagh* — Corner point.
29. **RINROE**: *Rinn Rúadh* — Red point.
30. **KILLASONA**: *Cill a' sonaidh* — Church of the mound, rampart or palisade.
31. **LISNANEANE**: *Lios na n-éan* — Fort of the birds.
32. **CASTLENUGENT**.
33. **TONYWARDEN**: *Tonn-uí-bhardain* — Barden's meadow marsh.
34. **ARDAGULLION**: *Ard a' Chuillin* — High ground of holly tree.
35. **ASNAGH**: *Easnach* — Trenched ground.
36. **TULLY**: *An Tulach* — Little hill.
37. **FERSKILL**: *A bhfeirscill* — Grassy field.
38. **LEITRIM**: *Liathdruim* — Grey ridge.

39. **AGHABOY**: *Acadh Buidhe* — Yellow field.
40. **COOLAGHERTY**: *Cul Eachartaigh* — Back of Arty's hill.
41. **MUCKERSTAFF**.
42. **BALLYMACROLLY**: *Baile mhic chruadhlaoich* — MacCrowley's town.
43. **WILLSBROOK**: — Formerly known as Monascreebe.
44. **GRAFFOGE**: *Graffóg* — Grubbed land.
45. **CLOONFIN**: *Cluain Fionn* — Fair lawn.
46. **BALLINLOUGH**: *Baile an locha* — Town of the lake.
47. **BUNLAGHEY**: *Bun na lathaighe* — Lower part of quagmire. In 1837 it was a village containing 65 dwellings and 299 inhabitants.
48. **HALFCARTRON**.
49. **CARTRONCAR**: *Cartrim na ceardhchan* — Cartron of forge.
50. **KILLINAWAS**: *Coill an amhais* — Soldier's wood.
51. **ROSSAN**: *Rossán* — Small wood, shrubbery.
52. **AUGHAMORE**: *Acadh mór* — Large field.

Local Placenames

Aghafadda
Aughatoom
Annagh
Anneville
Ardadolagh
Aughnasilla
Baker's Fort
Ballintrohan
Ballinanulty
Ballynamona
Ballynahowne
Barnarina
Blightoge
Boggaun
Bolie
Bornaringha
Cartronwillan
Carricknahoo
Carlisheen
Cartrongeeragh
Cealdrach
Corbaun
Corbet
Cornacosk
Cornethan
Cruckan, The
Cruckfee
Curraghduff
Deroragh
Droiched-na-gCailleach
Drumman
Drummilligan
Fernmount
Furry Park
Fooraun
Island, The
Killacroo
Knockslawne
Largan
Linagh
Lisbawn
Lisnabackerty
Lisnagree
Lisgaddery
Loughnagower
Maghera
Melkinagh
Milltown
Monoboll
Monascribagh
Monea
Moneen
Moorhill
Mossvale
Mullagh
O'Hara's Well
Orange Fort
Prospect
Ramoge
Rhine River
St. Patrick's Well
Shane Loonagh
Sherogh or Shrareaghan
Springpark
Terrenis
Tobergowna
Tooreknappagh
Tre-Sleamhan: *Field in townland of Clough, where the three parishes of Abbeylara, Colmcille and Granard meet.*
Walshe's Fort
Woodlands.

Trades

In the early part of this century, Granard was a hive of small industries, mostly conducted from people's own homes. In the Ball-Alley and Parnell Row, practically every home was engaged in a business of some sort. The Clyne family specialised in hand-knitted socks and crochet lace caps. The Carrs made baskets and cereals, and the Coyles were nailors. While Tracy was a thatcher, the Parks brothers were tailors, the Caddens painters, the Egans showmakers, and of the two Hannigan brothers, one was a surveyor and the other a builder, who built the Masonic Lodge on the Longford Road in 1890.

There were three blacksmiths' forges in the area, Nedleys, Dohertys and Staffords. Other forges in the town were Dohertys and McNallys in Barrack Street, but with the coming of mechanisation only one now remains, that of Gerry Flynn in Market Street. In Barrack Street also there was a tinsmith named Killala, and a coachbuilder named Matthews. Another coachbuilder named Fox lived in Market Street. Up until recent times a coopering business was carried on in Barrack Street by the late Andrew Smyth who annually exhibited and gave demonstrations of his work at the R.D.S. Spring Show.

R.D.S. 1946. Andy (RIP) and Rev. J. Smyth demonstrating their work as coopers.
Photo: Phil Smyth.

On Church Hill two families — Mulligans and Sheddocks — traded in religious goods and had stalls outside the Church during the annual two-week Mission. They also travelled over a wide area to wherever Missions were held.

In the timberyard on Moxham Street the late L. D. Kiernan employed a staff of carpenters and wheelwrights who turned out carts, coffins and furniture. Mr. Kiernan also provided a fleet of horse-drawn vehicles for ferrying goods to and from the town and Ballywillan Railway Station.

On Main Street there were two home confectioners — McGoverns and Dohertys. McGoverns also produced their own home-made sweets and a generous quantity in a cone-shaped paper bag could be had for one old penny.

At one time there were ten bakeries in Granard: Markey's, Devine's, Hayden's, Heslin's, Philip's, L. D. Kiernan's, P. M. Reilly's, Slevin's, Sheridan's and Regan's. Now only two exist — Devine's and Higgins'.

The only existing outlet in the area for home workers is St. Joseph's Knitwear Industry attached to the Convent of Mercy.

Leinster.   **GRANARD.**   **Pigot & Co.'s**

Extract from Directory, 1824
GENTRY AND CLERGY

Baker Jas. esq. J. P.
Barber Jas. esq, Moss-vale
Bell Andrew, esq, Creery
Burrowes Alex. esq, Ferraboro
Burrowes Lieut. Stephen, 5th Battalion
Dopping John, esq, Frankfort
Dopping Mrs. Ernehead-lodge
Edgeworth Major, Kilshrewly

Ennis Thos. esq, Paulis
Heldon Cornelius, esq, Bessville
Hinds Richd. esq, New Grove
Irwin John, esq, Ballinlough
Mc Canly Thos. esq, Keuroe
Nugent John, esq, Killasona
Robinson Rev. Dr. Fortland
Sheridan Rev. Geo. P. C.

Sheridan Rev. John P. P.
Thompson Major, Seneschal, Clonfinn
Thompson Rev. Geo. Clonfinn
Tuite Fran. esq, Higginstown
Tuite Thos. esq.
Webb Richd. esq, Lisryan
West John, esq, Castlenugent

MERCHANTS, TRADESMEN, &c.

APOTHECARIES.
Daly John
Kiernan Michael
Mc Cormick Hugh
O'Reilly John

BAKERS.
Ellis James
Gaffny Edward
Garron Michael
Graham John
O' Hanlon Patrick
Reilly Joseph

BOOT AND SHOE MAKERS
Brady John
Flood James
Friary Audrew
Gilcriest Patrick
Mc Caun Farrell
Mc Dermott John
Speer James

BREWER.
Major Thomas.

GROCERS.
Cahill George
Corcoran Peter
Daly John, (& spirit dealer)
Dogerty Thos.
Flanagan Margaret, (and spirit dealer)
Major Thos.
Mc Donnell Jas. (& spirit dealer)
Murtha Michael
Petit Patrick
Reilly Charles
Reilly Joseph

INNS.
Boyle James, (New Inn)
O'Hanlon Patrick, (Granard Inn)

IRONMONGERS
Corcoran Peter
Daly John
Mc Donnell James
Petit Patrick

LEATHER SELLERS
Fagan James
Major Thos.

LINEN & WOOLLEN DRAPERS.
Duuan John L.
Gevron Patrick, (linen only)
Mc Cann Ellen
Mc Kiernan Christopher
Murpha Michl. (linen only
O'Hanlon Pat. (by commission)
Phillips Michael
Reilly Pat. (linen only

PAINTERS AND GLAZIERS
Connell Patrick
Mc Donnell John
Tremble Robt. (& carpenter)

PHYSICIANS.
Daly Lieut. Mark Weatherly, E. and 2 Col. Dublin
Kiernan Michael
Mc Cormick Hugh

PUBLICANS.
Blake Wm.
Bryan Joseph
Carbry Susan
Dalton Edw.
Gaffney Edw.
Lynch Tereuce
Mc Cabe Bryan
Mc Donnell James
Moughan Patrick
Reilly Michael
Reilly Joseph
Reilly Philip

SADDLERS AND HARNESS MAKERS.
Dowd Charles
Sleavin Anthony

TAILORS
Donlan Patrick
Glynn John
Howracon Sumers
Masters John

TALLOW CHANDLERS.
Caffry James
Caffry Owen
Siggius Wm.

TANNER.
Feagan James

WATCH MAKER.
Kinlon Thos.

WHEELWRIGHTS.
Kenny Lawrence
Mackin Patrick
Murtagh Peter
Sheridan Patrick

WINE MERCHANTS
Daly John
Major Thos.

Miscellaneous.

Doherty Thos. calico dealer
Slator Edw. carpenter

COACHES

To Dublin on Mondays, Wednesdays, Fridays, at half-past six in the morning, and return to Granard on Tuesdays, Thursdays and Saturdays at 1 in the afternoon.

Transport

The accompanying map, which was produced by George Taylor and Andrew Skinner in 1778, shows the road route from Granard to Longford via St. Johnstown (Ballinalee). It is interesting to note the "Big Houses" along the way.

Granard also had a transport link with Dublin by Bianconi Coach. Garland's shop in Main Street was the site of the Coach House. The area had its highwaymen who stopped and robbed a coach at Lee's Hill between Granard and Abbeylara. In 1824 the Mail Coach departed for Dublin at 6.30am every Monday, Wednesday and Friday, returning on Tuesday, Thursday and Saturday at 2.00pm.

Ballywillan Station. *Photo: Ian White.*

In 1856-59 the Inny Junction Midland Great Western Railway line was laid down. The workers employed in the construction of this railroad worked an eight-hour day, six days a week for 4d per day. Around 1910 the third class single fare was 1d per mile. For a century Ballywillan Station, three miles from Granard off the Dundalk road, served the area until its closure in 1959.

Transport by road was boosted when, in 1927, two brothers Patrick and Thomas Donnelly, returned from America and founded the Pioneer Bus Service. Their transport enterprise flourished with buses linking Granard with Longford, Cavan, Mullingar, Athlone and Dublin. In 1967 Sean and Seamus Donnelly became the proprietors and continue this valuable service.

National Bus Service – operated for a year. G.S.R. Forerunner of CIE.   *Photo: T. Kiernan.*

A typical Donnelly's Bus in earlier days.   *Photo: Sean Donnelly.*

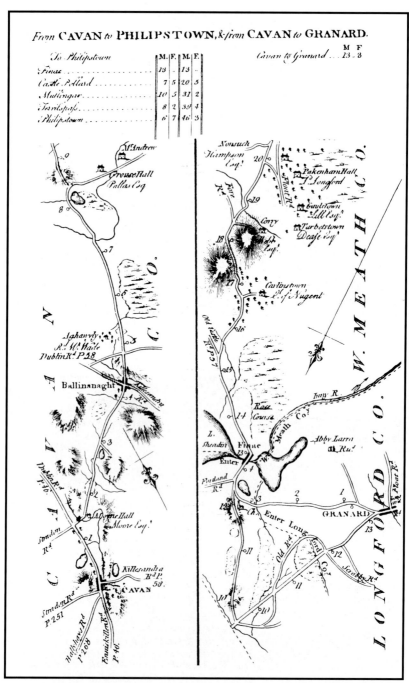

Map showing roads and 'Big Houses' in Granard area, 1778.

Flynn's Mills at Ballymacrolly

This ancient mill, with its Danish architecture dating back to the 11th century, came into the Flynn family about 200 hundred years ago. It has a long history. It is said that blood from those wounded at the Battle of Granard flowed into the stream forming the mill race. In the ordnance survey of 1837 it is recorded that "a mill pond, brewery, corn mill and corn kiln" were located here. For many years up to five tons of grain were transported from the mill into the Monday market in Granard and five hundredweight of grain was distributed to the poor of the town.

Flynn's Mills at Ballymacrolly. *Photo: Ian White.*

Threshing Song

We threshed in Ballymacroly today —
Some of us limber and lithe and gay,
Some of us seasoned and set and grey,
Men from four farms round the way
Helped at Ballymacroly today.

Oh! We set-to in Ballymacroly today —
Upwards the bundles we'd pitch and pelt
Cutting each beige or burnished belt,
And lodging the torrents of grainy wealth
In full-measured sacks in tiered array

At the threshing in Ballymacroly today
Old rusty-faced Barney was foreman of all,
He,d echo the threshers' turbulent call
For more shagged sheaves — with rasping bawl,
As he puffed his pipe with subtle delay!

'Twas under a sun of sober ray
That we threshed in Ballymacroly today;
But by light of a full harvest moon tonight,
When cleaned and collared (with pay packed tight),
We'll merrily race down Reillys' back flight,
And raise our glasses of froth-topp'd display
To the threshing at Ballymacroly today.

Laurette Kiernan, Greville Arms Hotel, November, 1945

Granard Creamery

This Creamery was sited in the vicinity of the present Granada Ballroom.

GRANARD CREAMERY (1903-1921) — Left to right: John Flynn, Trumra; Thomas S. Kiernan, Barrack Street; Miss Burnett, Miss Reynolds, Coolcor; M. Jennings, Asst. Manager, John Fagan, Charles Reilly, Creevy. *Photo: Mr. D. Kennedy.*

Creamery billhead. *Peggie O'Reilly.*

Granard Show Society

The Granard Show Society was founded in 1950. Dedicated committees have made the Annual Show one of the most successful in the Midlands.

COMMITTEE OF GRANARD SHOW, 1956 — Front row, l/r: Mrs. Kennedy, Mrs. Leonard, Mrs. Dunne, J. Flood, P. Briody, M. Tynan, J. Tynan, C.J. O'Reilly, D. Kennedy, Mrs. Daly, Mrs. Regan, Mrs. Moore, Miss Pettit. Second row: P. Small, F. Doherty, J. Ledwith, E. McGirr, J. Donoghue, P. Smyth, T. Devine, J. Tynan, J.P. Smyth, C. Fitzsimons, M. Kelly, J. Finnegan, J. Boyle. Third row: P. Flynn, E. Cunningham, J. Finnegan, B. Reilly, P. Flood, M. Bohan, T. Tynan, J. Leahy, W. Caldwell, R. Stephenson, J. Cunningham. Back row: R. Clancy, J. Lynch, J.J. Cunningham, P. McGivney, J. Duffy, J.V. Donohoe, E. Mullaney, P. Leavy, T. Kilbride, B. McGivney, H. Martin. *Photo: Mrs. P. O'Reilly.*

Fairs and Markets

Granard, the records tell us, is a small market town, and had in the present century, as an important part of its survival, the monthly cattle fairs and weekly markets. As well as a Fairgreen, there was a Hogmarket on Church Hill. A "spailpin hiring fair" was held on a Sunday in October at Granardkill Church, when the "Spailpins" with their spades arrived looking for seasonal work. Four annual fairs were also held in Bunlahy, the most noteworthy being the Gooseberry Fair on 26th July which continued to be held until 1934. Killgolagh Horse Fair, an important source of army horses, was held until 27th November, 1946.

"The first big pig fair was held on the fifteenth of January and the last pig fair of the year was held on 3rd May. At that time (about sixty years ago) five pounds was a big price for a pig."

May Fairs

On the First, Second, Third of May there were big fairs and a Hiring Fair the Monday after. Cattle from Roscommon used to come for the third of May and they'd bring their own hay with them.

There would be tents above on the green (in Granard) selling whiskey. Beside each tent would be a fire for boiling water to make punch which was a very popular drink at the time.

15th August

This was a big day in Granard and the place would be crowded and there'd be plenty of fights. There was always a big Cattle Fair. It started at five in the morning and would be over at about ten o'clock in the morning. It was a free day for the servant boys and girls and they would all be in Granard for the day, after First Mass. There would also be a contingent of police brought in for the day." *Recollections of B. Macken*

"What'll ye bid?" — Fair Day, Granard.   *Photo: L. McGahern.*

Never go to a fair where you have no business is an oul' saying and a wise saying. Padraic Colum hastens to add to this "that neither man nor mortal can be wise at all times". It was no surprise then that on the first Tuesday of every month the streets of the town came alive with wise men and foolish men, shrewd men and crazy men. They came from the neighbouring townlands and parishes and border counties to buy and sell or merely to observe.

The night before, the animals were moved to a front field. At three or four o'clock the following morning, after having been fortified by a mighty breakfast of strong tea, oven bread and several eggs, the farmers left home. The slow long journey, the tedious and maybe awkward bargaining, daunted no one and so they set their faces to the cold morning air and dewy countryside.

Earlier than nine o'clock found the army of men and beasts proudly ambling up the pavements and streets of the town. The town dwellers too had prepared, by erecting wooden barriers around their premises for fear that the cattle might wedge their way into doorways or windows.

Fairs were one of these occasions when anything in the world might happen. Here, whether he was young or old, the farmer had a veteran's knowledge of worth. He was born with this instinctive knowledge and wouldn't he want all his natural cunning for the jobbers who might try to 'do' him! First came the speculation, then a slow interest. Gradually the interest crescendoed into a passionate exchange of energetic bargaining. The animals were rapped in the hind quarters and ribs. Bargaining hands belted the air. The deal took place and was pledged by the customary spit on the hand, and the big interested crowd who gathered to witness the sale — like crows around a stook of oats — muttered approval or disapproval, as they deemed fit.

Once the bargain was struck both buyer and seller felt liberated and headed to celebrate their achievement. The Snug was the ideal place for conviviality and friendship. Here the air was drenched in an atmosphere of laughter, smoke and highspirited talk. Glasses clinked and were re-filled. Good humour abounded.

The markets, too, were scenes of rural extravaganza. The Christmas market on the 8th December was the culmination of many months' feeding and fattening for the Christmas dinner. It was the day of reaping for the womenfolk, who displayed notable quality in their poultry, eggs, butter and plants. The fowl would be plump and glossy with long yellow legs and pedigree as long as your arm. They blinked their eyes and cluck-clucked, totally unconcerned until they were caught by the legs for the weighing scales and consequent dispatch.

The prices following are reality — not make believe — and send ripples of nostalgia through the blood.

1914 — 1937		1914 — 1930	
3 year old cattle	£14 — £17	Pair of Boots	15/6d.
Yearlings	£11 — £14	1 oz. Tobacco	4d.
Calves	£3 — £4	Peggy's Leg	½d.
Cows	£18 — £28	Cigarettes	5 for 5d.
Fat Sheep	£3 — £5	1 pint Paraffin Oil	1d.
Farm Horses	£12 — £17		

1940 — 1960	
3 year old cattle	£28 — £47
Yearlings	£20 — £26
Calves	£5 — £8
Cows	£36 — £42
Fat Sheep	£6 — £8
Lambs	£5 — £6

1940 — 1960	
Pair of Shoes	25/-
1 oz. Tobacco	4d.
Suit of Clothes	25/-
Bag of Flour	50/-
Bag of Salt	10/-

The end of the Fairs –
the barricades come down.
Photo: L. McGahern.

THE END OF THE FAIRS

In the early 60's the old order changed and gave way to the new. The fairs were gradually replaced by the mart. Now in a well laid out premises complete with sales' rings, shelter, canteen and office facilities, the stock can be bought and sold in agreeable comfort.

Now the animal is like an examination candidate with a number and numerous certificates. Gone is the rising at 4 a.m. to begin the pilgrimatic journey — vanished too are the vendors or 'cheap Johns' (as they were called) who spread their speckled wares in the open air and sold with as much glamour and excitement as if it were a Christie's Auction in London! Like all things modern, the mart is a sign of the times, but it lacks — well — what we simply might call character and style.

Market House / Town Hall

Granard was granted the right by Charter to hold a market on Mondays and while we cannot say with certainty when the Market House was built, a building stood on the site in 1691.

Market House. *Photo: Mrs. C. Gillooly.*

The Market House was the hub of a busy market town. It was where grain crops were weighed, sacked and despatched by carters to the port of Drogheda for export. Produce for the home market included potatoes, eggs, butter, linen and vegetables. The crane yard and butter market were in close proximity. With the coming of the railways the carters went to Edgeworthstown station and later to Ballywillan. The Weighmaster in 1870 was John B. Kirk who lived in Fernmount.

Corn Market. *Photo: R.W. Stafford.*

Street markets declined gradually over the years. There are now only two held in December when turkeys are sold.

In 1979 the Market House reopened when the Granard branch of Country Markets was formed. A market is held in the lower portion of the building on Fridays.

The Market House played a role in the cultural tradition of Granard. In 1781, 1782 and 1785 Balls were held there. It is recorded that 1,000 people attended the Ball in 1785.

In 1826 Charles Carolan, R.C., taught a class of 14, in the upper room.

In 1921 the building was burned, but reopened in 1926. It was here that John McCormack sang; Anew McMaster brought Shakespearean productions; operas were performed and the local drama group entertained their townfolk. With the coming of electricity the Hall was used for three years as a cinema. Nowadays indoor games are played in the Hall, also it is the venue for Irish dancing classes and the annual Feis. It is a centre for activities during the annual Harp Festival.

The Petty Sessions were held every alternate week in the top storey of the Market House before a Magistrate. Since 1924 a monthly sitting of Granard Court is held before a District Justice.

Another section of the building includes the Town Clerk's Office where the Town Commissioners hold their monthly meetings. This room is also the office of Granard Credit Union.

In 1983 the Market House had a "facelift" and a very fine Branch Library was incorporated in the structure.

The Market House/Town Hall has indeed served Granard well.

Market Street. *Photo: Courtesy of the National Museum.*

Market Street, Granard

Pictorial record of Granard Market and women wearing shawls, which were a symbol of their married status – a custom which prevailed with some until the 'sixties. In 1837 it is recorded that the "women wore scarlet cloaks with hoods". *(Lewis Top.).*

Sport

Equestrian Events

Horses were highly regarded in Granard, particularly for sport. There was horse racing at Carrigy's of Robinstown and also in the fields behind The Rocks. The last steeplechase to be held at Bunlahy was on 27th March 1873.

THE BONLAHY STEEPLE CHASES

TO COME OFF
On Thursday, 27th **March, 1873**

STEWARDS:-

Alderman L. Reynolds, Esq. J.P.
John McManus, Esq. J.P.
John E. Thompson, Esq. J.P.
Clonfin.

R. A. Dopping Hempenstal, Esq. J.P.
Wm. Dobbyn, Esq. Abbeylara
L. P. Reynolds, Esq. J.P.

Judge – Thomas Bond, Esq. J.P.

Mr. John Sullivan, Treasurer and Secretary.

FIRST RACE

A Purse of Ten Pounds, weight for Age, 4 years old. 10st. 9 lb.; Five Years. 11st 7 lb.; Six Years old and Aged 12st. Horses that have ever won a Race, value £30 to carry 7lb. extra. Entrance 10s. to go to the Fund, and be paid to the Secretary on evening of the day before the Races, say 8 o'clock. Horses to be at the Post at 12 o'Clock. precisely. to start at Half-past 12 o'clock, about Two and a half-miles. 4 to Start, or no Race.

SECOND RACE

A Pony Race of 5 Sovs. for all Ponies belonging to Farmers in the Co. of Longford, and measuring over 14 1 Hands high. 5s. Entrance to go to the Fund Heats.

THIRD RACE

Farmers Race of First-class New Saddle, Bridle and Set of Horse Clothing. for Horses only belonging to Tenant Farmers of the Co. Longford. Horses that Started for the first Race not allowed to run in this Race. Heats: 4 to start or no Race.

FOURTH RACE

A Ladies' Purse for Beaten Horses, value to be declared on the Course.

RULES

The decision of the Stewards to be final and conclusive and Subject to no appeal.

The Race is to be run over a splendid Grass Course given by the spirited owners, to whom the Men of the County give their best thanks.

Printed at the Commercial Printing Office. Arvagh   Courtesy: J. Slevin

The Longford Harriers meet regularly in the area and on 1st January they meet in the town centre. Colonel D. L. Lefroy formed his own hunt and hunted the stag over his demesne, Carrigglas Manor. In 1860 the County Longford Hunt was formed as Harriers. At the end of the hunting season, Point-to-Point races were held for the enjoyment of the members and the farm owners over whose land they hunted. The present Master, Mr. Al McGuinness, Ballinree, Edgeworthstown, has held the office since 1954 and is the longest serving Master since the Hunt was formed.

Gymkhanas were held, on Ascension Thursday, the venues being the Convent Grounds or the Higginstown Estate.

Longford Harriers. *Photo: Al. McGuinness.*

Coursing

Coursing hares was a sport which was popular with some people and greyhounds were reared locally. Carrigy's of Robinstown provided the venue during the years 1932 to 1952.

Athletics

Cross country running was a big attraction. Races were held on the outer circle of the town. The starting point was "The Rocks" and from there to the back of the Motte, Rathcronan, on to the Workhouse and so back to "The Rocks". These events attracted many competitors.

Bullets

Bullets were played on the roads leading to the town. The game of "Bulletts" may have been introduced to the town by the Military who had come from Armagh or Cork where the game was popular. The bullet used could have been made of metal but was more likely to be a whin stone got from a local quarry.

One of the players usually tossed a coin to see which road they would choose on the day. Four players each had a round marble-shaped ball. Each player would start at a butt and then hurl the bullet as far as he was able. The place where it landed was marked. Some were able to throw it 80 perches. The game would continue for 3-4 miles. The owner of the first bullet home was declared the winner.

Horse Shoe Throwing
Horse shoe throwing was played on The Rocks. An iron bar was placed in the ground. The players would go back so many paces, each having three horse shoes. They woiuld throw one shoe at a time and try and put it round the iron bar. The best of three throws was the winner.

Skittles
Skittles were played by marking out a square. Each corner was valued five points, and the centre ten points. Six lengths of wood 12" long were hurled one at a time along the ground to knock the uprights. The player gaining 50-100 points was the winner. This sport was usually played in vacant lots or on footpaths.

Hurling
The local name was 'Commons'. Hurling was played with a hurling stick which was more or less like the hockey stick of today. It was made from whin, ash, blackthorn or apple tree. They were called caimín sticks. Great value was set on a straight whin with a bent end. The ball was a solid piece of wood, smaller than the hurling ball of today. Two stones or coats were used as goal posts. The game could last for hours. One goal generally won the game. It was played in the Convent grounds and in the field beside Markey's Barns which is just opposite the new sports complex. Granard hurlers won the County Championship in 1932 and 1934.

Members of Granard Hurley Club 1932. Back row, left to right: James Sheridan, Padge "Padna" McNally, Tommy Kiernan, Big Dan. Front row: Terry Sheridan, Christy Brogan.   *Photo: T. Kiernan.*

Badminton

A thriving badminton club existed in the town for many years, the venue being the Town Hall. Teams played in various leagues throughout the Midlands. This was a most sociable and successful club and was noted for its great hospitality to visiting teams. After a lapse of a few years the game is now being played in the new Community Centre.

Football

Football was played with a ball made from straw, hay or "sprat" grass. It was played in the Convent grounds, Markey's Barns and Carrigy's of Robinstown from 1920 to 1965. Granard was represented in the 1880 Championship by a team called "Granard Healy's". Granard Slashers was affiliated in 1891. Granard won the Junior Championship Final in 1927. In the period 1929—35 Granard contested seven Senior Championship finals, losing only one in 1932.

1914   Senior Championship
1927   Junior Championship
1928   Junior Championship
1929   Senior Championship
1930   Senior Championship
1931   Senior Championship
1933   Senior Championship

GRANARD TEAM 1925 — Back row: P. Carters, W. Daly (RIP), J. Gavigan (RIP), J. Macken, T. Finnan (RIP), P. Dale (RIP).
Middle row: F. Smith (RIP), M. Daly (RIP), J. Regan, C. Brady, T. Smith (RIP).
Front row: T. Sheridan (RIP), P. Sheridan (RIP), J. Clynes (RIP), P. Daly (RIP).
Two young boys: Brian Dale and Martin Daly.   *Photo: J. Regan.*

1934 Senior Championship
1935 Senior Championship
1941 Senior Championship
1955 Minor Championship, Schools' League
1956 Minor Championship
1957 Juvenile Championship, Schools' Championship
1958 Schools' Championship, Juvenile Championship, Schools' League, Junior Championship
1960 Minor 9-a-side, Schools' Championship, Schools' League, Minor Championship
1961 Juvenile Championship, Schools' Championship Granard Senior Tournament
1962 Schools' Championship, Ardagh Senior Tournament, Granard Senior Tournament
1963 Juvenile Championship, Ardagh Tournament,
1964 Leader Cup, Minor Championship, Juvenile 9-a-side
1965 Minor 9-a-side, Minor Championship
1966 Senior Championship, Cornafean Tournament, Leader Cup, Special Senior League
1967 Senior Championship, Minor League
1968 Cornafean Tournament, Junior League, Schools' League, Delvin Tournament
Three U-21 Championships—1966, 1967, 1968
1969 Leader Cup, Junior League, Special Senior League
1970 Senior Championship, Under 21 Championship
1972 Senior 9-a-side
1973 Cornafean Tournament
1976 Intermediate League, Junior League
1978 Junior League, Minor 9-a-side
1979 Under 21 9-a-side
1980 Cornafean Tournament, Under 21 9-a-side, League Div. II, Under 14 Championship
1981 Cornafean Tournament
1982 Senior Championship, Senior 'B' Championship
1983 Schools' Championship (Urban)
1984 Schools' Championship, Schools' League (Urban)

Tennis

During the 1930s and subsequent years, there was a vibrant tennis club in Granard, the court being situated off Barrack Lane. Travel was difficult due to petrol restrictions but this did not deter the players from arranging 'away' matches. On trusty bicycles they rode to neighbouring clubs in Longford town, Castlepollard, Oldcastle, Ballyjamesduff and Virginia. They played their match, partook of refreshments and thought nothing of riding the return journey singing a song to shorten the road.

Handball

Handball was played extensively using a small firm ball, made of rubber. It was played against gable walls of houses mostly on Parnell Row. There was a Ball Alley in the area behind the Barracks.

Tug-o-War

1933 KILLASONNA TUG-'O'-WAR TEAM — Back row, from left: Christopher Reynolds, Ballboy (RIP), Eugene Masterson, Coldoney (RIP), Jimmy Lynch, Ballywillian, Willie Sheridan, Robbinstown (RIP) and James Reid, Killasonna. Front row: Michael Dunleavy, Killasonna (RIP), Pad Briody, Killasonna, James Burke (trainer) Granard, James O'Hara, Killasonna and James Brady, Rinchola.
Photo: Courtesy Longford Leader.

Members of the Kilbride family, Cartron, continue to take part in this sport.

Ploughing Matches

Though ploughing matches were not strictly sporting events, they were very much a social occasion with the farming community. In the Granard area tillage was a popular farming exercise. Farmers prided themselves on their skill in turning the sod. The venue for ploughing matches was Carrigy's of Robinstown. It was here, in 1954, that the Fordson Major Tractor was first demonstrated in Ireland, heralding a new era in farming.

Pitch and Toss

Pitch and Toss was played with two or more players. A medium sized stone called a spud was placed on the ground. The players stood behind a line, throwing the pennies to the spud – 'pitch'. The two pennies nearest the spud were placed on a flat piece of wood and tossed into the air — this of course was called 'toss', the two owners calling heads or tails as the coins were tossed into the air. This action was repeated until the pennies came down both heads or harps. At intervals someone would be heard saying "Flick the pennies, clear the spud, evens all round".

Sleighing

Sleighing was indeed the highlight of the winter months. The snow became hard packed on the hill leading to the Motte and young people drawing sleighs behind them made their way to the top of the hill. The sleigh was made from timber and iron, held in place with strapping of tin.

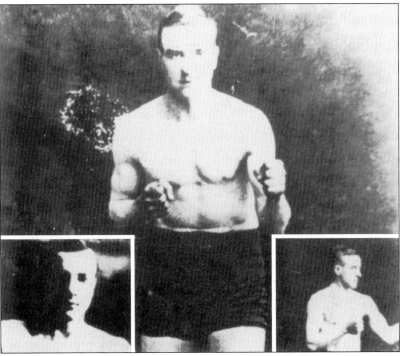

Edward O'Reilly – Ned the Piper from Coolarty, worked in Belfast and boxed as a 'welter weight'. *Photo: T. Kiernan.*

Folklore

Captain Bland was attached to the Cavalry Regiment in Granard in the late 18th century. He was killed when he jumped his horse over the Barrack wall.

This poem is in the collection of the (Folklore Department – University College, Dublin).

Captain Bland

The midnight hour is striking
The gates are open wide
Four headless steeds come prancing out
Four headless men astride
And at their heels, a shining coach
Rolls lightly o'er the sand
And, in the coach, a headless man
Well known as "Captain Bland".

As quick as light a'down the town
Where howling mongrels hide
Round Markey's turn, the Dublin Road
Before them opens wide.
Down Tor Mhin Hill, the whips are cracked
Like signals of command
By Creamers Fort, and Brennan's dam
The coach of "Captain Bland".

Old Barrack Wall.   *Photo: T. Kiernan.*

By Abbeylara's ancient walls
Where monks in bygone days
Had made the Abbey cloisters ring
With songs of prayer and praise.
By old Kilbride and Ballinacross
'Tis rolling swift and grand
Up Barrack Street, by Cronan's Fort
The coach of "Captain Bland".

The Barrack gates still open wide
The steeds prance in once more
The gates are shut and all is still
The midnight ride is o'er.
But old men say that troubles great
Come quickly on our land
Whene'er the headless horsemen drive
The coach of "Captain Bland".

Stories of '98

Big Pat Farrell
Pat Farrell from Ballinaree, Edgeworthstown was the biggest man in Longford, being over 6 feet tall. He led the Longford rebels into Granard. When it was decided to attack the Barracks they advanced over the fields by 'the rocks' and jumped their horses into the Barrack yard. It was a death trap. Pat Farrell was the first leader to fall, shot through the heart by Dopping Hempenstall. His mare "Black Bess" made her way home to Ballinree riderless. In 1924 roadworkers discovered the skeleton of a man in the townland of Asnagh where it is said Pat Farrell had been buried.

Willie O'Keefe
Willie O'Keefe, either from Ballinlough or Culvin, Streete, and his men halted at the top of the hill of Ballinagall where a council of war was held. They advanced and fought in the Barrack yard. When the retreat was sounded, O'Keefe made the superb jump over the wall — the last man to escape from there with his life. He outrode the Redcoats through Ballymorris. He went to Donore Lake and rode his mare across the lough to an island where he let the mare out to graze. The Meehan family lived on the island. He took refuge in an outhouse behind a wooden plough. At nightfall he heard the shout — "There's O'Keefe's mare! He must be here." Two yeomen prodded the wooden mould boards of the plough with their swords and said "He's not there", and so he escaped. He was five years "on his keeping" and there was £500 on his head, but he was never

House at Pipers Cross. *Photo: Ian White.*

Thatched Cottage. *Photo: Ian White.*

caught. His property was confiscated in 1803 by Spools of Kilteevan House. The O'Keefe family moved to Winetown, Rathowen.

Stories told by Thomas and Richard Monahan. Willie O'Keefe was their great, great grand uncle.

Alex and Hans Denniston

The Denniston family were Presbyterians who farmed at Prospect, Granard. They also imported from America flax seed to be grown locally. Should the flax crop fail, the Dennistons could have been sued.

Records show that in 1796 Alex Denniston was Second Lieutenant in the Mostrim Cavalry of Yeomanry. He and his brother Hans became members of the United Irishmen.

The Denniston family have in their possession a faded letter dated 23rd November 1796, in which there is a reference to the unrest at that time.

Dear Brother

. . . which has a risen a good deal of disturbance. There were many taken prisoner in Belfast and went to Newgate in Dublin persons of property . . . shortly quelled.

The Summer Assizes of 1798 record that "Hans Denniston for assault against John Beatty, Alex Denniston for assault and felony against Patrick Smyth — True Bill in each case." They must have been acquitted, for they fought at Granard in September. Hans went to Belfast to consult with the Ulster Directory of the United Irishmen re strategy for Granard.

A letter from a yeoman officer who fought at Granard says that "the rebels appeared with muskets and pikes commanded by Alexander Denniston, Mr. Hans Denniston, Mr. O'Connell and Mr. Miles O'Reilly, all of this neighbourhood."

When they realised that to continue fighting was futile the retreat was sounded by Hans Denniston. Alex on his white horse headed west, evaded capture, reached Westport where a branch of the family lived and from there escaped to America. Hans escaped across the Hill of Molly. When he looked back from the hill he could see his house burning.

Hans, while he was an outlaw, reached the house of a relative in Drumnacross, Clonbroney. While a meal was being prepared, yeomen came searching for him. He evaded capture by hiding in a holly bush which still grows at the house.

Later Hans was not so fortunate, as he was captured and imprisoned in Kilmainham Jail. The following entry is taken from the Kilmainham General Register:

No. Name	When Committed	By whom
117 Hans Deniston	18 Sept. 1803	Secretary Wickham
Crimes	**When discharged and by whom**	
Treasonable Practices	Sec. Wickham on 3 Dec 1803	
Place of Abode	**Remarks**	
Longford		

Hans is also considered to have gone to America. There is no record to show that the brothers returned. Their names are not recorded in the family burial ground in Old Clonbroney.

The Denniston house at Prospect was burned down in 1920.

This information courtesy of Mrs. Susan Forster (nee Denniston), Ballinalee.

The Battle of Granard
A Ballad recorded from oral tradition by Peadar Ó Duigneáin

Air: "The   Rising   of   the   Moon"

Down by Sheelin's vale at sunset
 Fierce as demons in their wrath.
Spread a band of English troopers
 Fire and carnage marked their path.

Midnight shines, and blazing rooftree
 Lit the darkness of the night
From the shores of fair Lough Gowna
 To the slopes of Granard's height.

Maid and mother fell before them
 All in wrath and vengeance smote,
And in pride the foeman's legion
 Onward sped to Granard's Moat.

We marched that morn from Creenagh
 To oppose them on their way,
And by river, lake, or mountain
 Made we neither stop or stay.

Till a band of English troopers
 Crossed our path at Edgeworthstown
And we piked the last red foeman
 As the evening sun went down

Early in the dewy morning
 As the day began to dawn
Towards the ancient moat of Granard
 We were proudly marching on.

For a moment's space we halted
 As we came within their view
Then a deadly thirst for vengeance
 Filled our bosoms through and through.

With a shout that loudly echoed
 To the far-off Shannon shore,
Through the red ranks of the foeman
 In a furious rush we tore.

With that rush our gallant pikemen
 Leaped against their foremost line
And their blades drank deep in vengeance
 For many a bloody crime.

Fast and deadly ev'ry weapon
 Found a Saxon foeman's breast
As our fierce and maddened pikemen
 Through their columns thickly pressed.

Granard's ancient moat was reddened
 By the blood of friend and foe
Well we met them with their bayonets
 With our pike their sabre-blow

Backwards pressed agains the valley
 Bravely fighting to the last,
But again our gallant pikemen
 Gathered round them fierce and fast.

High o'erhead us waved our banner
  In its beauty fair and free
Borne by men from Carrickmoira
  And the plains of Killashee

From the banks of Cloonart river
  And from Cleaney's village green
Hast'ning onwards to the onset
  Many a gallant youth was seen.

As we reached the heights of Granard
  Right before us, formed in line,
We could see the English legion
  And their spears and banner shine.

Morning saw their haughty standard
  In its pride and glory wave;
Evening saw the foeman's legion
  Crushed and sunk in one red grave.

And where stood the ranks of Britain
  By the light of morning's dawn
O'er their graves in proud defiance
  Erin's rebel banner shone.

Longford long shall tell the story
  How her children bravely stood
In that fight for Erin's glory
  Brave and stern as freemen should.

And their deeds shall nerve their brothers
  When they grasp the freeman's brand
To go forth, to fall or conquer
  For the rights of motherland.

'98 Memorial

There are croppy graves in Ballinagall, Gallid, Clough, Carrigduff, Ballygilchrist and the plot on Church Hill.

The Famine

"The year before the Famine there was an enormous crop of potatoes and when they had the spring seed taken out of them, they hadn't enough pigs to give them to and they wouldn't give them to the cows. The surplus potatoes were left at the backs of the ditches and they all rotted.

"A lot of people died during the Famine. My grandfather had a farm at Granardkill during the Famine time. The graveyard was only a couple of fields over from my grandfather's place.

"It was the winter of the Famine year and this man was working with my grandfather. He was a workman and was a cranky class of a man.

"A lot of people were a buryin' this day and my grandfather made the remark to a workman, 'God bless us', he says, 'how many times have I heard that bell today!' He was talking about the chapel bell ringing for all the funerals.

"The fellow says, 'Now is the time to bury them when the ground is soft.'

"My grandfather was so angry at the fellow's callous remark that he ran him and would not employ him. The next week the workman was a burying himself.

"Public Works: The big hill at Brown's Cross was lowered as a public works. The hill was sunk and put in the hollow. My mother was goin' to school at that time and remembers the hill a levellin'.

"If there was a couple or three sons in a house only two would be employed on the public works out of the three. They would get a couple of shillings a week and a portion of Indian meal."

This story was told by Bernard Macken, farmer, born and reared in Granard. He was 80 years old in 1935.

J. Delaney — Dept. of Irish Folklore

"Nightmare"

William Carleton (1794-1869) novelist, recalled his journey from Ulster to Munster as a "Poor Scholar". He spent a night in Grehan's Inn, Main St., where he had such a bad dream that, next day, he retraced his footsteps northwards.

The Cave of Diarmuid and Grainne
is in a limestone rock in a field locally known as "the Rocks" near Granard. Tradition has it that Diarmuid and Grainne took shelter in this cave during their elopement.

Stray Sods
There are numerous "Stray Sods" in the Granard area. It is said that if a person steps on one of the sods between sunset and sunrise he would be unable to find his way out of the field. These "sods" are located in fields near Springtown, Rinroe, Mullinroe and Purth. To break the spell

of the 'Stray Sod' — the traveller had to remove his coat and turn it inside out before finding his way out of the field.

The Hungry Grass

Legend has it that should anybody walk on "The Hungry Grass" they developed an insatiable appetite. This "Grass" is supposed to cover the resting place of those who died in famine times, hence the great hunger.

The Big Wind

On the 6th January, 1839 a stranger arrived in Granard. Some thought he was a sailor. He warned the people of an approaching storm and advised them to tighten the ropes on the hay reeks and corn stacks. He also told them to quench the fire on the hearth — raking fires was then the custom. Many heeded the warning. When the storm broke, Lee's house on the Abbeylara Road was the only one in the area to catch fire. There was no loss of life. The stranger was never seen again in the area.

The Coole Trotter

The Coole Trotter was famous all over Granard. He was a huge black dog that had red eyes and a fiery mouth and feet that made the noise of a horse's feet trotting. His red eyes and fiery mouth gave him a fierce look.

He started off at Mill's Lane. He followed down the hill, down by the Mart, out by the dump to Killasonna and out the Bog Road to Coole, in by Cammagh Bridge and through Abbeylara and back into Granard and up Moxham Street. By now he had covered all the town and he ended at the Barrack Gate at 12.00 most nights, especially on Hallowe'en night.

Any young person who saw the Coole Trotter would die young and any old person who saw him would have bad luck for the rest of his life.

– Paul Howard (age 8).

Tobar Righ an Domhnaigh (Tobereendoney)

Tobar Righ an Domhnaigh (Tobereendoney) — See Holy Wells. The following stories about this 'Well' are recorded by O'Donovan:-

Not many years ago, a dry summer caused all the neighbouring wells to disappear and the natives thought that this 'King of the Waters' would be so propitious as to allow its waters to be drunk by cattle and used in making butter and in washing and boiling potatoes. But they were mistaken: for it is contrary to the nature of sanctity to allow itself to be turned to any profane use. Their cattle died and a plague was observed to proceed 'from the use of its waters!'

It is also told that a poor man who stood in need of fire, cut down some branches off the trees growing over this well, and brought them home

A Granard Family at turn of 20th century.

to his wife, telling her that he would not want fire while there was a single branch over Tobereendoney. But when the wife learned where the bundle of branches were found — she would not burn them and told her husband that he had been guilty of a very sacrilegious act. The poor man took this to heart and fell into a decline, which carried him off in a few months. Notwithstanding the awful sanctity of this well, it does not appear that it was ever blessed by any Saint, nor is it known from what source it derives its sanctity.

Stations may be performed at it with great benefit on any Sunday in the year, because it is dedicated to the King of that day — i.e. I suppose to God, the King and Lord of every day and night as well as Sunday.

Cures

Chin Cough / Whooping Cough
(a) Ferret's Leavings: Take milk to a Ferret, let it drink its fill — the patient must drink the leavings for the cure.
(b) Drink mare's milk.
(c) The leavings from a meal of a married couple who share the same surname.

Mumps
Put an ass's winkers on the child's head and lead it by the reins three times around the pig sty or across a stream. As an alternative take a silk stocking filled with heated salt and put around the patient's neck.

Thrush
Bring affected child to a person born after the death of his/her father. This person will breathe into the child's mouth nine times and say a prayer. The thrush will disappear.

Stone Bruise
Bathe foot in a bog hole. Let two people stand one either side of you. Throw stones from each side across foot and throw away the ninth stone.

Warts
(a) Get a black snail without looking for it. Rub on warts and then hang on whitethorn bush. As the snail withers the warts will disappear.
(b) Rub warts with fasting spit for nine successive mornings.
(c) Dip the wart into the water on a blacksmith's trough where he has cooled the irons. In the name of the Holy Trinity. Repeat on following two days. Each visit to be at sunset.

Boils
(a) Point the edge of a knife or hatchet three times.
(b) Eat herb – plantain and boil will disappear.

Wildfire (Skin rash)
Rub with gold on Monday, Thursday and Monday – three times each day in name of Holy Trinity.

Headache
A person who has never seen his father cures a headache by placing his hands on sufferer's head. If hair is cut on Good Friday — no headache for 12 months.

Strain (Sprain)
(a) Two visits necessary to person with "the cure of the strain". Cure involves tying a thread or piece of string around the strain and saying a prayer. This cure is handed from mother to son *or* father to daughter.
(b) Pull the leg and say out loud "abhaile leat", "abhaile leat! man goin' over the bog bring the strain with you."

Burns
A person to acquire the cure must get a "mankeeper" and lick it on back, belly and sides. He will lick the burn and be cured.

Mankeeper.

Ringworm
Rub with gold on Monday or Tuesday — three times each day and say a prayer in honour of Holy Trinity. It is widely known that the seventh son has this cure.

Shingles
At first sign visit the person with cure and bring him some home-made unsalted butter. The person with the cure bleeds his own finger and lets the blood fall on the butter. The patient takes home this butter and rubs it on the affected part.

Stye of Eye
(a) Get someone to say to you "You've a stye in your eye" nine times, after each announcement you reply "You're a liar" and the stye will go away.
(b) Get nine gooseberry thorns, point eight of them at the stye and throw the ninth across the right shoulder.

Chilblains
(a) Rub with snow.
(b) Steep feet in warm urine and chilblains will disappear.

Jaundice
(a) Ferret's leavings, as for Chin Cough.
(b) A secret herb recipe done locally.

Common Cold
Boil buttermilk, when it curdles, strain, drink hot liquid (whey) with sugar and lemon before going to bed.

Wasp Sting
Rub with redshank leaf or household vinegar.

Bee Sting
The blue bag or any alkaline, e.g. bread soda.

To prevent bleeding on damaged animal horn
Cover damaged stump with spider's web.

Sore Throat
Wrap neck with a scarf or ribbon which had been left out of doors on the eve of St. Brigid's Day.

Georgian Doorway.

Photo: Ian White.

"Piseogs"

Signs

Weather

Good
(a) Smoke going up straight from the chimney.
(b) A red sky at night, a shepherd's delight.
(c) Cattle on the hill top.

Bad
(d) Cattle under a ditch.
(e) Horse with his back to the wind.
(f) Curlews cry.

Visitors Coming
(a) Laying hen or dog with a straw on tail.
(b) If lice come into the house.
(c) If a knife falls off the table.

Ill Luck
(a) If you break a mirror (seven years).
(b) Never cut a lone bush.
(c) It is unlucky to interfere with a fairy fort.

Good Luck
(a) If two people say the same thing together, you are due a letter.
(b) If sparks leap out of the fire, money is coming your way.
(c) If you care for a stray cat, good luck will follow.

Creevy House. *Photo: F. Murtagh.*

Entertainment

Granard was, and still is, a town full of music and talent. When they were not putting on their own shows, the people flocked to see and support the travelling players who came to town. Anew McMaster considered Granard to have one of the most discriminating and discerning audience in the Country. He played Shakespeare and other classical theatre for many years to a packed and hushed hall.

All entertainment was announced by the bell ringer or town crier — the best remembered being Joe Kelly.

Count John McCormack sang at a concert in the Town Hall on January the 6th 1912. Among his solos were *"I'm sitting on a stile Mary"* and *"Carrickdoon"*. Later in the evening he sang in a trio with the late Barney Macken, and the late James O'Reilly. He was accompanied by Mrs. Margaret Cosgrove (nèe Slevin) — for fifty years the church organist at St. Mary's Church, Granard.

Other famous personalities who sang in the Town Hall were Josef Locke, Martin Crosbie and Maire Ní Scolaidhe, the noted traditional Irish singer.

Travelling dramatic troupes were frequent visitors to the Town Hall. Included in these were Anew McMaster, Louis D'alton, P. Daniels and the Comerfords.

Some members of the local drama group in 1948 — left to right: R.W. Cassidy, H. Smith, T. Kiernan and Phil Smith, in a scene from one of their many productions.

Amateur dramatics played a big part in the town's Cultural life. Plays staged included *"The Rising of the Moon"*, *Riders to the Sea*, *Murder in the Red Barn*, *Willie Reilly and his Colleen Bawn* and *The Money doesn't Matter*. T. P. McKenna a younger banker, who went on to star on stage, screen and television joined with the local dramatic society during his time in Granard.

Interval music was played by the local quartet: Eily Flood - Piano, James O'Reilly - 1st Violin and the Misses Dorothy and Dolly Pettit - Cello and 2nd Violin.

For most of these plays and concerts, an adequate stage was erected of timber from the undertaking firm next door, and the piano was carried from the home of Mrs. Margaret Cosgrove.

Margaret Hayes of Granardkille, a violinist of international repute, also performed in her home town. She went on to play for many years with the London Philharmonic Orchestra, and has performed with touring chamber orchestras throughout the world. She is also a soloist of note.

Percy French is reputed to have stayed at Kiernans Pub in Bunlahy, where he was inspired to write *"Whistlin' Phil McHugh"*.

In 1933 Padraic Columb, the poet, also featured the area in his book *"The Big Tree of Bunlahy"* subtitled *"Stories of my own Country Side"*. His song *"She moved through the Fair"* also refers to the locality.

In the Town Hall in the 1930's Larry Cogrove had a film show on Sundays. Here we saw for the first time the movie-picture, and the red plush tip-up seats of the future.

In the 1940's the McDonald and McEvoy families established the Alpha Cinema in Barracks Street. Long queues lined up outside the building to see the top ranking films.

In the early 50's the famed Granada ballroom was established by Tommy Kiernan and the late Tommy Quinn. This legendary dancehall brought young people to the town in their thousands to dance to all the major "big bands". It still stands today, in all its glory and is used for a variety of events.

St. Mary's Abbey, Abbeylara.

Brass and Reed Band

The Brass and Reed Band disbanded in 1914 when the "call to arms sounded". Some of the members of the Band were Harry McGill, Thomas and Philip Cadden, John, Pat and James McNally, Ned Smith, Bernard and Frank Creegan, Patrick Cunan, Pat Regan, Frank Coyle, Bernard McAllister, P. Parkes. The drummer was John Carters 'Parnell'. The Band Master Philip (Reynard) Klein, a German, was married to a local girl, Jane Stafford.

Accordeon Band

In the days before the Harp Festival was revived in Granard there was an accordeon band. Members of the band in this recently re-discovered picture from 1937, back row, left to right: Bernard Columb (RIP), John Maguire (RIP), Joe Regan, Joe McCormack (RIP), James Kiernan and Thomas Flaherty. Middle row: Willie Daly, Michael Reilly (RIP), Marty Daly (RIP) and Patrick "Copsy" Daly (RIP). Front row: Denis Flynn (RIP), Paddy Carters and Pat Kelly. *Photo: J. Regan.*

Con Kiernan, Ferriskill, a motor cycle enthusiast, built a "Wall of Death" in which to practice stunts. This gave a film producer the inspiration for the film *Eat the Peach* which has received such acclaim.

BETHANY TO CALVARY — Successfully produced at Granard, Longford and Oldcastle by St. Mary's Dramatic Guild, Granard, 1935. In the front row are Fr. Sheerin (RIP) and Fr. McCormack (RIP), who were Curates at St. Mary's at the time. Included in the cast are Mary and Nan Macken, Bridie Macken, Julia Macken, Kathleen Regan (RIP), Chrissie Regan, Maggie Cosgrove, Sybil Curran, May Shaughnessy, Mollie Geraghty, Babs Connell, Teresa Daly, Nano Brady, Rosemond and Dolly Pettit, Winnie Reilly, Mrs. Tom Brady (RIP), Jim Regan, Bernard Columb (RIP), John Monaghan (RIP), Joe Smyth, Michael Farrell, Thomas Flaherty, Johnny Rogers, Johnny O'Hara (RIP), Leonard McGrath NT (RIP), Brian Brady (RIP), Joe Pettit (RIP) (Francis Coyle), Ned Kelly and Peter Donoghue (RIP).
Photo: E. Regan.

"The Harper's Land"

In 1981 the bi-centenary of the first Harp Festival was celebrated. A committee under the chairmanship of late Canon Francis Gilfillan, worked enthusiastically to make the festival an annual event and so revived interest in harp music.

Canon Francis Gilfillan.
Photo: Ian White.

Granard's contribution to harp music was recognised in America when *The Harper's Land* album by Ann Heymann and Alison Kinnaird, was recently released.

Ann Heymann comes from Minnesota and is recognised as the foremost exponent of the wire-strung harp. Ann plays her harp in the old Irish manner on her left shoulder and plucks the strings with her nails, which are grown long. She won the Grand Prize at the Bun Fhleadh Harp competition in Granard in 1981 and 1982.

Alison Kinnaird comes from near Edinburgh and she plays the gut-string harp in the Scottish tradition.

Both these fine players combined their talents and the result is an album of traditional and original airs.

The Granard tunes are: –
(a) 'Carraic na h-Uaine'
   a legendary landmark in the area.
(b) The Market House
   the scene of the Harp Festivals in 1781, '82 and '85.
(c) John Dungan's Return
   refers to the Granard businessman who lived in Copenhagen and

sponsored the Festival and was present in Granard in 1885.
(d) The Canon's Cup
refers to the trophy sponsored by Canon Francis Gilfillan and won by Ann Heymann in 1981 and 1982.

Group of Harpists.   *Photo: J. Donoghue*

GRACE NUGENT

MISS FETHERSTON or CAROLAN'S DEVOTION

Granard in the Eighties

The population of Granard now (1987) stands at over 1,600. Since the nineteen sixties many new families arrived in Granard and built new homes on the outskirts of the town. The County Council have built over seventy modern houses in Denniston Park and Tromra Road thus solving the housing problem in the area. Two new reservoirs have been installed.

Business and agricultural enterprises gradually integrated to bring increasing prosperity to Granard:

Five factories on the outskirts of the town produce lingerie, joinery, animal foods, insulation material and credit card imprint machines. A new Garda Station was built in 1975. The old Parochial House has been converted to a business premises. The Greville Arms Hotel has been refurbished throughout.

Among the many business establishments are included five hairdressing salons; four butchers; five drapers; two large supermarkets; pharmacy; numerous family grocers and licensed premises; restaurants and take aways; a large furniture emporium; builders providers; hardware and electrical stores; engineering works; garages; agricultural suppliers and a smithy. Two bakeries supply bread and confectionery throughout the country. The financial needs of the town are catered for by two Banks, a Credit Union and two Building Societies.

The Chamber of Commerce has helped to assist many of the above and to attract more business to the town.

The two secondary schools have been extended to educate over 800 pupils from the catchment area.

Sport and leisure complexes are included in the Higginstown Estate for outdoor and the Community Centre for indoor activities.

Wednesday is a particularly busy day in Granard when the Farmers' Mart holds its weekly auction. Additional sales held on several Mondays throughout the year together with the Granard Country Market are the only reminders of the old Market days.

We, the people of Granard, while keeping our heritage alive, face the future with confidence —

"Le súil ar an aimsir atá imithe agus ag súil leis an aimsir atá romhainn."

Granard's History & Heritage continues to unfold

2002

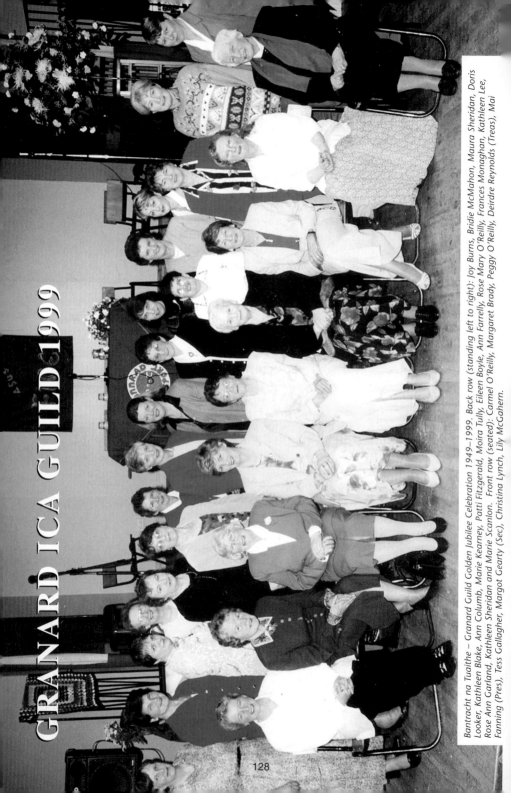

Bantracht na Tuaithe – Granard Guild Golden Jubilee Celebration 1949–1999. Back row (standing left to right): Joy Burns, Bridie McMahon, Maura Sheridan, Doris Looker, Kathleen Blake, Ann Columb, Marie Kearney, Patti Fitzgerald, Moira Tully, Eileen Boyle, Ann Farrelly, Rose Mary O'Reilly, Frances Monaghan, Kathleen Lee, Rose Ann Garland, Kathleen Sheridan and Marie Scanlon. Front row (seated): Carmel O'Reilly, Margaret Brady, Peggy O'Reilly, Deirdre Reynolds (Treas), Mai Fanning (Pres), Tess Gallagher, Margot Gearty (Sec), Christina Lynch, Lily McGahern.

The 2002 Excavation at Granardkill, Co. Longford
by Kieran O'Conor and Mary Dillon

INTRODUCTION

In the wet and windy early spring of 1999 archaeologists from Duchas (including one of the present writers who then worked for that organisation) surveyed the remains of what appears to be a deserted village at Granardkill (Mon. No. LF010-078). This complex lies about one kilometre to the west of Granard, adjacent to the town graveyard. It is held that the medieval parish church of Granard was also located at Granardkill (Bradley, Halpin and King 1985, 19). The earthworks of this deserted village site extend over several acres. Up to twenty-five possible house- and hut-sites, a number of rectangular-, wedge- and D-shaped enclosures, some ridge-and-furrow and various grassed-over streets and roadways can still be seen. It is widely believed that these earthworks at Granardkill represent the remains of a borough (presumably never more than an agricultural village in physical terms) set up by Richard de Tuite, the Anglo-Norman lord of Granard, at some stage in the early 13th century (e.g. Bradley, Halpin and King 1985, 15-17).

There are certain problems with this interpretation. A motte castle is located beside the present town of Granard and this seems to have been built by Richard de Tuite in 1199, probably on and within a pre-existing ringfort. This earthwork, which is located on the highest point in Granard, is clearly one of the finest examples of this type of castle in Ireland. A motte can be described as a great mound of earth whose flat summit would have held wooden and cob-walled buildings and defences. Sometimes a defended enclosure known as a bailey was attached onto its base. It is clear at Granard that the supposed pre-existing ringfort was modified by de Tuite and turned into a bailey. Again, the defences surmounting the banks of a bailey and the

Crutch-headed pin of 11th or early 12th century date found at Granardkill.

buildings within it were also usually built of timber or clay and timber. Basically a motte-and-bailey, like the one at Granard, was a castle constructed of earth and wood, rather than of stone. Up to five hundred mottes may have been built by the Anglo-Normans in Ireland during the course of the late 12th and 13th century (O'Conor 1998, 18). Interestingly, another of the country's most spectacular mottes also occurs in Co. Longford. This is the motte at Lissardowlin, which lies outside Longford town on the main Edgeworthstown road. This motte actually has two baileys adjacent to it and again appears to have been constructed on a pre-existing ringfort (Orpen 1910). Anyway, the motte built by de Tuite at Granard in 1199 was to act as the centre of his lands in the area, acting as a residence, administrative centre and fortress.

LACK OF PROTECTION

It seems strange that the associated borough of this castle with its English-speaking inhabitants would have been placed at Granardkill about one kilometre to the west of the motte. It would be expected that this ancillary settlement would have been built beside the motte for protection, especially as Longford was a frontier area that saw much warfare between the Anglo-Normans and the Gaelic Irish. Furthermore there is some historical evidence to suggest that the earthworks at Granardkill were located on church property right throughout the later medieval period and not on de Tuite land (K. Nicholls, UCC, pers. comm.). This is important as it appears that during the whole later medieval period many Gaelic-Irish laymen opted for settling on church land, as such places were less liable to attack in comparison to secular settlements (Nicholls 1987, 403). It is possible, therefore, that the earthworks at Granardkill could represent the remains of a Gaelic-Irish settlement of general 12th-century to 17th-century date located on church land for protection against the violence of the times.

There is another possible explanation for the deserted settlement at Granardkill. The farmstead beside the graveyard and deserted village earthworks, owned by Pat Sheridan today, is marked 'Granard Castle' on certain editions of the six-inch Ordnance map for the area. It has been suggested that this site may mark the location of a castle (possibly a tower house) built by William O'Farrell in 1405 (Bradley, Halpin and King 1985, 18, 20). Again, the various historical, literary and cartographic sources suggest that small nucleated settlements occurred beside Gaelic tower houses and lordly residences in the 16th century for protection against the endemic violence of the period. This would mean that the earthworks at Granardkill could possibly represent the remains of such a late medieval settlement – being possibly abandoned in the 17th century with the break up of the Gaelic system.

The only problem with this particular interpretation is that there is no physical evidence for a tower house on this site today and nor was there in the 19th century. The site is not marked 'Granard Castle' on the 1st edition of the Ordnance Survey map which came out in the late 1830's. A small gentry house (of which a photograph survives) was built here sometime in the late 19th century. This house was demolished in the early 1950's. A castle is always a good address – be it in the 13th century or 19th century! It is just possible that the builders of this edifice decided to call their house 'Granard Castle' in the late 19th century and this would explain the name – in turn meaning that there was never a tower house at this site.

In all, therefore, there are a number of options as to what the remains of the deserted village at Granardkill actually represents in terms of function, dating and ethnicity.

THE 2002 EXCAVATION

Clearly the main question for the excavation surely was to date the earthworks of the deserted village at Granardkill. For example, do the earthworks there represent the remains of the Anglo-Norman borough set up by Richard de Tuite around 1200? Alternatively, are they late medieval in date and instead represent the remains of a nucleated Gaelic Irish settlement located for reasons of security on either church land or beside a tower house?

In June of 2002 a team of archaeologists and students mainly from NUI, Galway and the University of Florida started to excavate the site in what again was wet and windy weather. The excavation lasted about five weeks in all, with the main work being carried out in the first four. Three areas of the site were targeted for excavation. These will now be discussed in turn.

Work in progress on the dig.　　　　　　　　　　　　　　　*Photo: Bríd White.*

Aerial photograph of the Granard area featuring raised areas.

Photo: Kieran O'Conor.

TRENCH 1

A 20m long by 3m wide trench was cut across two rectangular embanked enclosures in what is really the middle of the site. There were two particular questions for excavation to answer here. Firstly, at what date was the bank that separates the two enclosures constructed? In other words, at what general date were the two enclosures erected and formed? Secondly, did the two enclosures function purely as agricultural fields or were they the courtyards of houses with evidence of habitation within them?

The excavation of this part of the site indicated that the bank was mainly constructed of earth but may have been revetted on its northern side by a dry-stone wall. Some pottery finds within the bank suggest a 16th- to 17th-century date for its construction. A ditch was uncovered along the whole northern base of this bank. The ditch was clearly part of a system that funnelled rainwater into what appears to be a pond further to the west. There is no natural source of water on the site and, presumably, the settlement's cattle and other stock needed to be watered on a daily basis. The field evidence from the Duchas plan suggests that permanent water sources were made three different low-lying places on the site. The field evidence for silted-up drains and the excavated drain from Trench 1 indicates how these ponds were kept filled with water. A find of an early clay-pipe fragment suggests that the drain silted up or was deliberately filled in at some stage in the 17th century.

There was no evidence for houses or occupation in these two enclosures cut by Trench 1. Instead, they appear to have functioned as fields apparently in the 16th and 17th century. Again, very faint cultivation ridges were visible before excavation in the northernmost of these enclosures, suggesting that this small field was cultivated – growing either grain or vegetables originally. The southernmost enclosure or field had no evidence of furrows within it. The soil here was not deep in the way that it is in the northern enclosure. This southern field may have functioned as a stock enclosure.

NEARLY TEN THOUSAND YEARS

It must be remembered that the Irish countryside has been occupied for nearly ten thousand years. Each generation has made its mark upon the landscape. In this respect, there are a number of prehistoric burial and ritual monuments dating to the Neolithic (c. 4000BC – c. 2500), Bronze Age (c 2500BC – 500BC) and Iron Age (c.500BC – 400AD) occur in the vicinity of Granard (see Warrilow 1998). These include the henge at Ballybrien, the ring barrow at Ballymore and the stone circles at Cloghchurnel and Cartronbore. Some form of prehistoric enclosure occurs across the road from the site itself in the field beside Pat Sheridan's house. The whole Granard area was clearly well settled in prehistoric times. Actual evidence of this prehistoric activity was found during the course of the excavation.

At the southern end of Trench 1 at Granardkill a stone-lined pit with deposits of cremated human bone was discovered. This pit is characteristic of stone-lined pit burials of the Bronze Age. There is a huge variety in the burial ritual of this time. The dead were most commonly placed in either stone-lined pits or cists (stone coffins) and these were sometimes covered with a cairn or earthen mound. Pit graves vary from being large oval or sub-rectangular in shape with crouched inhumations to small circular pits with cremated bone deposits. Some pit graves are very simple with no stones at all, others have just a few randomly placed stones, some are paved, while others again are covered with a slab (Waddell 1990, 16). As such graves often yield exciting artefacts there was huge anticipation on site as to what we might find. Various types of pottery bowls, vases and urns are the most common grave goods of the Bronze Age and turn up in even the simplest of pit burials. Sometimes metal objects are found in these graves. For example, silver earrings were found with a female inhumation in a pit burial at Rosnaree, Co. Meath (Waddell 1990, 21). Flint knives, arrow heads and scrapers along with stone axe-heads are also relatively common finds, as are bone objects, especially bone pins (Waddell 1990, 21-25).

The sides of the grave at Granardkill were lined with upright stones and at the bottom lay one particularly large flat paving stone, which had smaller stones encircling it. The sides of the grave were very straight and sharp and the base was rounded. There were five layers of deposition and all of the layers contained some cremated bone and unburnt cattle bone. The greatest amount of cremated bone was found mixed with charcoal and was lying on the paving stone. Most of the cattle bone was recovered from beneath the stones. The large amounts of cattle bone in the pit could be indicative of the funeral feasting that we associate with this era. One of the uprights in the grave was found to be some type of grinding stone, evident from its smooth, worn face and the shallow hollow worked into its centre. Bronze Age people may have used it, along with a rubbing stone, for grinding grains or for some other domestic purpose. Or perhaps it was used to reduce the cremated bone into the tiny pieces we found it in? Worked stones of domestic purpose have been found before in Bronze Age graves, e.g. a saddle quern was discovered in a cist burial in Carrower in Co. Mayo where it was used as one of the side stones in the cist (Waddell 1990, 118). We must remember that any amount of organic material, whether placed as grave–goods or used in the construction of the grave, could have been present but obviously would not have survived. For example in one cist at Ballybrew, Co-Wicklow, traces of rush matting were found, seen in the encrustation of the carbonate lime on one of the paving slabs of the cist (Waddell 1990, 27).

What does this grave tell us about Bronze Age activity in the Granard area? There is a large possibility that the Granardkill grave is part of a cemetery given that Bronze Age pit and cist burials most often occur in groups of two or three. Even groups of over forty burials are known e.g. at Mound of Hostages on Tara, Co. Meath. About half of all cist and pit graves were found on their own but this is most likely due to a lack of excavation in the surrounding area (Waddell 1990, 27-29). Even given the fact that this grave at Granardkill is likely to be accompanied by other graves, only some of the community could have been buried here and this points towards a hierarchal society.

TRENCH 2
Trench 2 lay on the western side of the site. A 3m wide, 10m long trench was dug across the interior of one of the embanked enclosures. This particular enclosure had the remains of cultivation ridges just visible to the naked eye within it. The aim of this part of the excavation was, like Trench 1, to try to figure out what this enclosure was when it was in use.

There were no traces of any domestic occupation in this enclosure. A fine plough soil, with some sherds of pottery of 16th- and 17th-century and clay-pipe fragments mixed within it, which went right down to the natural subsoil, was uncovered in this trench. This suggests that the enclosure functioned as a small, tilled field originally, with the visible cultivation ridges being contemporary with it. The suggestion from the pottery sherds found within the plough soil (which were placed there as part of a manuring process) is that this enclosure was worked and presumably built at some stage during the 16th and 17th century.

Nevertheless, a number of furrows were found cut into the subsoil in this trench. These lie on a different alignment to both the enclosure and the plough furrows visible to the naked eye. They are clearly earlier in date to the enclosure but it is impossible to say when they were formed as no finds came from them. All that can be said is that they seem to be evidence for agricultural activity at Granardkill prior to building of the village and its fields.

Anyway, the main importance of the work carried out in Trench 2 was that showed that the enclosure here was not the courtyard of a house. It merely functioned as a small tilled field growing grain or vegetables for the settlement at Granardkill during the course of the 16th and 17th century.

THE HOUSE AREA
One of the grassed-over remains of a building within the village was chosen for excavation. This feature lay on the north-eastern side of the site. The remains here before excavation consisted of a rectangular area defined by low banks – clearly the remnants of some sort of house. It was an extremely difficult area to excavate, simply because the stratigraphy here proved to be extremely complex. The excavation indicated that the walls of the house were probably constructed of sods and stone, much like modern field banks in the Granard area today. Clearly these walls were not load-bearing and could not have carried the weight of the roof. Instead, it is possible that the roof of this building was supported by cruck-trusses. The rafters and thatch of this structure may have been placed on pairs of large, usually curving timbers (called crucks) joined at roof level. This means that the walls of this house did not carry the heavy weight of its roof and acted as weatherproofing only. The finds from the house seem to indicate a 17th-century date for its occupation.

Aerial photograph of the Granard area with ring forts.

Photo: Kieran O'Conor.

The south-western side of the house was built over a pre-existing ditch. This ditch was clearly filled in immediately prior to the erection of the latter structure. It is unclear when this ditch was originally formed and this is clearly a question for future excavation at the site.

POST-MEDIEVAL FINDS

A cobbled area was created around the house and over part of this ditch. Again, finds of post-medieval date were found within this area indicating that it functioned as part of a courtyard around the house. One find of early medieval date, however, was found in this area. This was a bronze crutch-headed pin and was used as a dress fastener. Such pins were in use in Ireland from the early 11th century though to c. 1150 (O Rahilly 1998, 26). This pin was clearly earlier than the layer it was found in. Nevertheless, its existence shows occupation of the site in pre-Norman times. This is also confirmed by the existence of two round-headed sandstone window heads still to be seen in the two niches on either side of the entranceway to the modern graveyard at Granardkill. These seem to have been from a stone church that was built at Granardkill sometime in the 10th, 11th and 12th century and of which nothing now remains above ground level. A monastic site existed at Granard (presumably Granardkill) from the beginning of the early medieval period and this early church was associated with St. Patrick (Bradley, Halpin and King 1985, 15). Presumably the stone church evidenced by the stone windows in the entrance to the modern graveyard at Granardkill replaced earlier wooden churches on the site. The historical evidence and the stone windows from an early church confirm that there was early medieval activity on the site.

CONCLUSIONS AND SUMMARY

What was achieved by the 2002 excavation at Granardkill? It must be remembered that dig itself only really lasted for about a month and clearly more work is needed at the site over the next couple of years. Nevertheless, the excavation did produce some interesting results. It would appear on available evidence that the deserted settlement at Granardkill, as it now appears with its grassed-over house sites, fields and roadways, dates to the 16th and 17th century. The visible surface remains at Granardkill really do seem to date to the latter two centuries and are not 13th century in date. The excavation produced no evidence of 13th- or 14th-century activity on the site. No structures were uncovered or artefacts were found that belong to the Anglo-Norman period. The available evidence, therefore, suggest that the deserted village site at Granardkill was not the site of the borough set up by de Tuite in the 13th century and presumably deserted in the next century due to military pressure from the Gaelic Irish. It must be presumed at present that this Anglo-Norman borough was located somewhere beside the motte, close to modern Granard.

When was the settlement at Granardkill deserted? Again, as noted, the excavation suggests a broad 16th- and 17th- date for the earthworks. The

Ordnance Survey antiquarian John O'Donovan, writing in the 1830's, stated that the settlement at Granardkill was deliberately abandoned 'after the Battle of Aughrim'. Presumably this statement was based on folk memory in the Granard area at that time. This statement by O'Donovan suggests a date in the 1690's or even just after 1700 for the abandonment of Granardkill as a settlement.

The excavation also indicated that the embanked enclosures at Granardkill were not the courtyard of houses but simple fields. The dig also allowed an understanding of the way artificial ponds for watering livestock were created in places across the site. Simply, information was gathered about the way space was used within the settlement when it was occupied during the 16th and 17th century.

The overall evidence also hints that the site was an important church site in early medieval times. The really unexpected result of the excavation was the uncovering of the prehistoric (probably Bronze Age) pit burial with its cremation. This is yet more evidence to show that the Granard area was heavily settled in prehistoric times. It is a reminder that the landscape around Granard has been farmed for thousands of years. Presumably other pit burials occur in the vicinity of the one at Granardkill.

In all, given the short length of the excavation, much of interest was uncovered during it. It must also be stated that the hospitality and friendship shown to the Galway and Florida students by the people of Granard and its environs was magnificent. Hopefully these students will always remember Granard with affection throughout their lives, despite the wet weather of June 2002.

BIBLIOGRAPHY

Bradley, J., Halpin, A. and King, H. 1985 *Urban Archaeological Survey – County Longford* (limited distribution). Office of Public Works, Dublin.

Nicholls, K. W. 1987 Gaelic society and economy in the High Middle Ages. In A. Cosgrove (ed.), *A new history of Ireland, vol. II, medieval Ireland, 1169-1534*, 397-438. Oxford.

O'Conor, K. D. 1998 *The archaeology of medieval rural settlement in Ireland*. Dublin.

Orpen, G. H. 1910 The mote of Lissardowlin. Co. Longford. *Journal of the Royal Society of Antiquaries of Ireland* 40, 223-5.

O Rahilly, C. 1998 A classification of bronze stick-pins from the Dublin excavations 1962-72. In C. Manning (ed.), *Dublin and beyond the Pale*, 23-34. Dublin.

Waddell, J. 1990 *The Bronze Age burials of Ireland*. Galway.

Warrilow, S. 1998 *Granard's standing stones*. Longford.

By Dr. Kieran O'Conor, National University of Ireland, Galway
and Mary Dillon, Associate.

Maps of the Granard area

Irish cartographic history starts in the 16th century when Elizabethan planters introduced large scale mapping as a useful way of recording the extent of land in Ireland. One of the earliest maps for the Granard area is of the Barony of Granard in Co. Longford, presented to Sir Robert Cotton before 24th February, 1630 by James Ware (see copy inside back cover). Maps of a high aesthetic standard were rare in Ireland before the 1750s, which saw the arrival to the country of two innovative mapmakers, John Rocque and Bernard Scale, who developed what is generally called their "French School" of cartography here. Thomas Sherrard and John Brownrigg are recorded as Scale's apprentices and were responsible for a succession of partnerships, which transmitted their master's legacy into the 19th century. The maps produced are now part of the Longfield Collection in the National Library of Ireland, which contains a number of sheets relating to Co. Longford (NLI 21.F.4:16-29). Several of the maps, produced in the 1790s by or on behalf of John Brownrigg, depict townlands in the baronies of Ardagh and Granard.

Probably most worthy of mention in the context of County Longford is the Edgeworth collection of maps, produced in the early 19th century by Richard Lovell Edgeworth and his son William. In 1809 R.L. Edgeworth was a member of a government commission set up to examine the peat bogs of Ireland. Maps were produced at a scale of 4 inches to the mile showing the course of rivers, soil type, drains, roads and any features, which might be considered as part of conversion of wet land into dry. Towers, raths and hilltops also appear on the maps for use as convenient markers for trigonometrical operations. One such feature is shown on top of Granard moat in the form of a small square with a path leading from it.

In 1813 William Edgeworth produced five barony maps for Granard, Longford, Moydow, Rathcline and Shrule which, in 1814, he amalgamated into the Grand Jury Map of the county (Scale c.1 inch to the mile). These maps aimed to give a clear and attractive picture of relief, water, roads and principal buildings. Townland names, mills, churches, antiquities and houses in dot form are all shown. Particular attention is given to the physical features of the maps. The intricate river, lake and forestry patterns weave in and out of the extremely detailed relief features, depicted schematically by dense hachuring.

The Ordnance Survey, established in 1824 at the Phoenix Park, Dublin, was initially set up to deal with land valuation in Ireland. In order to collect the county cess efficiently it was necessary to know the exact acreage and valuation of every townland in the country. The Director of Surveys for Ireland, Major Thomas Colby, was an efficient organiser. By 1846, with the aid of 2,400 officers, Colby had achieved more than he had been directed to do. Not only were the townlands delineated but the topographical features within the boundaries were also mapped out. .This material was enhanced by the work done by John O'Donovan and Eugene O'Curry who recorded

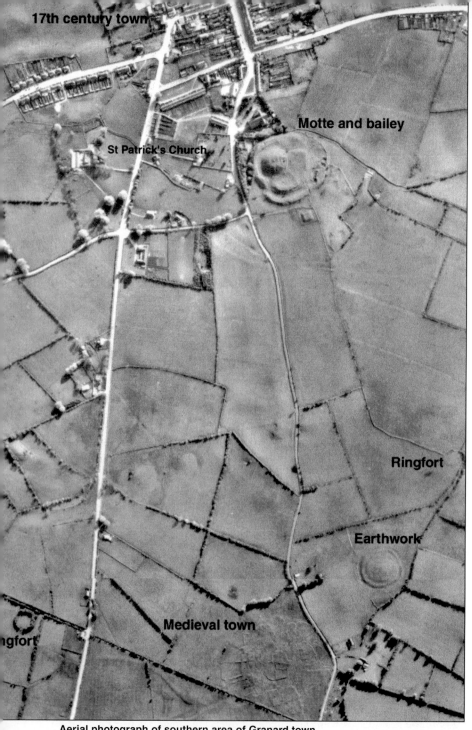

Aerial photograph of southern area of Granard town.
Source: Ordnance Survey of Ireland – No. 611019 and 611017.   *Supplied by: Sarah Gearty.*

the place names and antiquities of the countryside for the Ordnance Survey from 1829-40. This turned the townland survey into a document recording thousands of years of cultural, archaeological and historical life, and not just a record of mid 19th century land use and ownership.

Alongside the six inch Townland Survey, the Ordnance produced a series of town plans at the scale of 5 feet to 1 mile (1:1056). Granard and Longford were both mapped in 1836 and these plans survive in manuscript form in the National Archives, Dublin. Similarly, in conjunction with the General Valuation of Ireland (Griffiths Valuation) of 1830-1858, a series of high quality hand drawn town plans was produced. These maps cover the whole county and most of them are also at the scale of 5 feet to 1 mile. In County Longford town plans were drawn for Abbeylara, Ballymahon, Granard, Kenagh, Lanesborough and Longford.

In Ballymacroly townland, near Granard, 17 buildings are distinguishable including two "mills". Forts are shown with the use of hachuring. Roads, rivers, bridges and fords are detailed. The collection also includes an excellent town plan of Granard. The moat, barracks, (St. Patricks) church, a pound (on the hill) and the fairgreen are all depicted. Houses on Main Street total 59 and a key gives the name of each occupant.

Cartographic records such as those mentioned above offer a rich and varied source of historical information as they trace the development of each area of the county's landscape for over three centuries.

Source: Maps of County Longford, 1790-1840 – Sarah Gearty from Teathbha, Vol. II No. 4 (1997) Longford Historical Journal.

MEMBERS OF RED CROSS UNIT, GRANARD – AUGUST 1943 — included are Mary Kate Reynolds, Nan Lynch, Nan Macken, Kitty McLoughlin, Nuala Cosgrove, Dolly Pettit, Mary Pettit, ___ Dolan, May Donohoe, Lily McLoughlin, Bob Geelan, Tim McGahern, Eilish Killeen, Tommy Kiernan, Mrs. Killeen, Dorothy Pettit.
Photo: Courtesy of Nan Macken.

Useful map sources for Granard

Maps showing Granard and its surrounding area

'The barony of Granard in the County of Longford', c.1618 (British Library, Cotton MSS). [Note date].

* Down Survey barony map of Granard, c.1654.

Longfield collection of maps, c.1790 (National Library of Ireland, 21.F.40:16-29).

* Grand Jury map of the barony of Granard, 1813, by William Edgeworth.

Bog Commission map, district no. 7, Longford and Westmeath, 1810, by R.L. Edgeworth (National Library of Ireland).

Municipal boundary map, Granard. In *Municipal corporation boundaries (Ireland) reports and plans*. HC 1837 (301), xxix. (National Library of Ireland).

Ordnance Survey, map of County Longford, 1:10560 or six inches to the mile, sheet 10, first edition, 1837.*

Ordnance Survey, map of County Longford, 1:10560 or six inches to the mile, sheet 10, second edition, 1913.

Ordnance Survey, map of County Longford, 1:2500, sheet 10:12, 1913.

Large scale maps showing Granard town

Ordnance Survey, map of Granard, 1:1056 or five foot to the mile, 1835 (NAI OS140).

Valuation Map, Granard, 1:1056 or five foot to the mile, 1841 (Valuation Office, Ely Place, Dublin).

Also probably should mention ...

Ordnance Survey memoirs and namebooks.*

* = in Longford County Library but please check all with Mary Reynolds.

Sarah Gearty, M.A., Cartographic Editor, Royal Irish Academy.

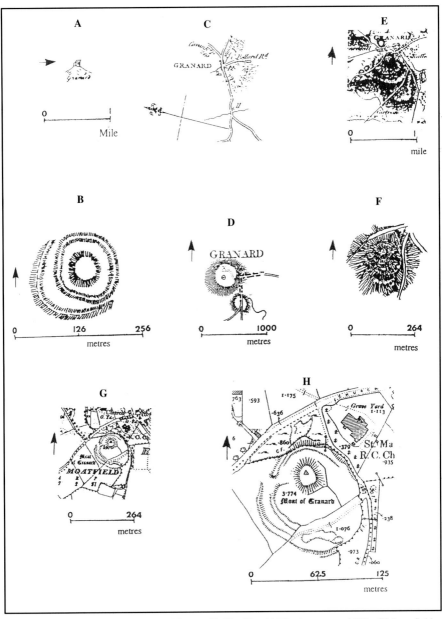

The **'Moat of Granard', Site 13: A)** Ware's map, ca. 1630. **B)** Longfield map of Granard, ca. 1790. **C)** Maps of the Roads of Ireland, 1778.
D) Bog Commission map, 1810. **E)** Grand Jury map, 1813.
F) First edition OS map, 1913. **H)** 1:2500 OS plan, 1913.

Courtesy: Sarah Gearty.

Aerial photograph of the Granard area.

Kieran O'Conor.

The Motte
— further reflections

(See also related text on pages 5, 28 and 35)

The striking appearance of the Motte and Bailey at Granard has been of interest to travellers for many centuries. J.C. Curwin, in 1818, *Observations on the State of Ireland, Vol. II* commented — 'the castle, built on a surrounding hill rising to a considerable height ... as the surrounding is perfectly flat, the hill has the appearance of a work of art.'

The enigmatic origin of this Motte has posed questions for many researchers. Is it the remains from the 5th century of the site of the residence of Caibre, son of Niall of the Nine Hostages? Was it where St. Partrick was received by Caibre when he, Patrick, came to Caibre Gabhra? Is the Motte and Bailey a Norman construction? The present-day great mound could have been constructed by the Normans who would have had the necessary engineering skills to build such a mound. The Annals of Loch Ce record in 1199 – 'the castle of Granard was built this year.' In 1172, when Henry II landed in Wexford, he granted the kingdom of Meath to Hugh de Lacy. The kingdom comprised the present counties of Meath, Longford, Westmeath, parts of Dublin, Kildare and Offaly. Notes by Philip Mac Dermot in *The Annals of Ireland* state that, in return for the ancient kingdom of Meath, De Lacy was to supply Henry with 50 Knights. Richard Tuite came to Ireland "in the suite of the Earl of Chepstow, he was early selected by Hugh de Lacy as one whose character would maintain the marches of his Palantinate, even in their most advanced and assailable situation; he accordingly received from that nobleman an extensive tract in the district of Teffia, the most westward portion of Meath." Granard, though still in Irish hands, would have been included in King Henry's grant.*

The Motte appears to have been a strategic military base for both the English and native Irish during the intervening centuries, ownership alternating between the two. It was a very important look-out during the Battle of Granard in 1798.

With such a chequered history, it will not be until extensive excavations have been carried out that the Motte may give up more of its secrets. It is the impressive appearance and mystical quality of this mound that has led, not only to several written commentaries on 'Granard Moat', and to its inclusion on many early maps.

Michael Collins, while in London on the Treaty negotiations in 1921, took time off on his birthday, October 16th to write to his fiancée, Kitty Kiernan:

"How I wish I was there now – on the Moat. Last time I was on the Moat, early morning. Do you remember? I looked across the Inny to Derryvarragh, over Kinale and Sheelin (and thought of Fergus O'Farrell) to Mountnugent and, turning westward, saw Cairnhill where the beacons were lighted to announce to the men of Longford that the French had landed in Killala...."

* *Source: Garland, Kieron, The Moat of Granard – project-essay for the Trinity College Schools Prize in History, 1997.*
    Additional material by J. Burns and B. Grier.

Archaeological Sites around Granard

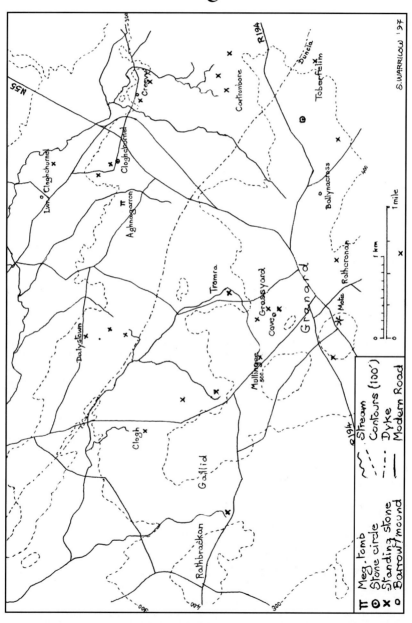

Details of Sites in the Granard area

SITE LOCATION	REF.	O.S. MAP REF.	OPW REF.	Ht./Lgth.	Wdth.	Thick.	Orient.	Ht. ASL
Clogh	1	31608323	10/20	151 cm.	44 cm.	29 cm	/	355'
Clogh SE	26	321 830	/	130	112	41	0°	380'
Dalystown N	2	32768398	10/110	140	36	31	/	335'
Dalystown (destr.)	3	32728379	10/111	NK	NK	NK	NK	325'
Dalystown E	4	32848367	10/19	125	151	22	75°E	320'
Dalystown S	5	326 835	/	64	79	28	21°E	325'
Lwr. Cloghchurnel	6	34858437	7/501	150	105	47	60°E	280'
Lwr. Clogh'nel (fallen)	7	348 843	7/502	193	135	30	NK	280'
Lwr. Clogh'nel (reset)	8	348 843	/	109	168	30	NK	280'
Cloghchurnel	10	34808364	/	140	128	48	0°	380'
Cloghchurnel (fallen)	9	34738375	/	148	60	46	NK	360'
Creevy	11	35638327	11/10	201	132	38	133°	310'
Creevy E.	22	358 832	/	101	117	58	151°	306'
Cartronbore W.	13	35768220	11/13	117	85	32	114°	370'
Cartronbore E.	14	36198217	11/14	120	86	52	NK	365'
Cartronbore (destr.)	12	35928229	/	97	87	67	108°	365'
Ballynacross	15	35118071	/	79	91	54	118°	410'
Tromra	16	33278211	/	118	110	34	50°E	390'
Mullingee	17	32508183	/	94	100	30	136°	470'
Grassyard W.	18	32988182	/	118	32	20	50°E	455'
Grassyard E.	19	33088170	/	120	38	13	140°	460'
Grassyard SE.	20	33078157	/	104	56	23	36°E	470'
Rathcronan	21	33688072	/	107	106	25	48°E	420'
Toberfelim	23	360 811	/	114	79	61	60°E	385'
Higginstown	24	338 799	/	102	38	26	40°E	400'
Granardkill (fallen)	25	325 807	/	181	33	23	NK	490'
Tromra W.	27	326 825	/	108	183	61	55°E	385'
Aghnagarron	A	34408351	11/04	121	85	38	52°E	385'
Cloghurnel Circle	B	34908356	11/07					
Cartronbore Circle	C	35378125	11/16					
Grassyard Cave	D	33008161	10/112					
Ballynacross mound	F	34488102	11/15					
Cloghurnel barrow	G	34478451	7/04					
Creevy barrow	H	35708330	11/08					
Granard Mote	E	32988072	10/8001					

by Stephen Warrilow,
Graduate,
Bristol University.

Lake Settlements in Lough Kinale

In 2002 new investigations around the lake settlements in and around Lough Kinale (cf. p.79) and Derragh Lough (cf. p.34/35 and map p.79) commenced. This area was formely investigated by the Crannog Archaeology Project (CAP) in co-operation with the National Museum of Ireland due to the finding of for example an ornate 8th century Book-Shrine (cf. p.34/35) during illegal treasure-hunting activities in these lakes. A tree-ring date suggested that the crannog in Toneymore North was extended and used in the early 12th century. Studies in Insular art and archaeology, 81-98). The waters were also surveyed in the summer of 2001 by the Crannog Research Programme on behalf of Duchas the heritage service and results will appear in the forthcoming Longford survey volume.

The aim of the Discovery Programme's activities in this area is to learn more about how people addressed lakes and waters at different points in time by analysing and interpreting primarily the archaeological material, but we will also take help of environmental sciences to get a better understanding of among other things the vegetational history of the area and the study of maps and place-names. The most monumental expression of people's activities on lakes are of-course the crannogs and in the study area there are three distinct crannogs, or man-made islands. These islands would have been constructed by making a circular arrangement of posts in the water and filling up the interior with stones, planks and other debris. Crannogs would have been used as settlements and it is not unusual to find remains of small huts on them. There are indications that people may have lived on the lake in the later Mesolithic period. During the summer of 2002, the Lake-Settlement project cooperated with Duchas Underwater Unit and their divers managed to identify that the crannogs in this area seems to have been built also by the placing of quite substantial radiating timbers making out a series of super-imposed platforms. On top of these platforms were later on piled building-masses and what remains today may be interpreted as house remains. We managed to retrieve samples from these platforms on all crannogs and look forward to dating results

Crannog in Derragh Lake.

from these. If these samples are suitable for tree-ring dating we may be able to discuss if these three sites were constructed in sequence or if they were the result of one singular event.

With the help of a detailed shoreline and water survey we managed to locate a good collection of stone-tools that now are undergoing analysis to help us to understand people's lives on the lake during early pre-history. These were located at what appears as an island between the waters of Kinale and the bog at Derragh td. What we already know today is that people in these times favoured spatially distinct places such as natural islands and our environmental analysis will tell if this place at Derragh td. was an island in the past. Our IT-team has also made great progress in the detailed mapping of earlier shorelines in this area, together with the surface of the crannogs discussed above. Our field-survey team has also walked the whole shoreline and managed to find an extension of the Black Pig's Race stretching further down around the southern half of Lough Kinale than was formerly known. The results will be published by the Discovery Programme.

Dr. Christina Fredengren
Assistant Director
The Lake Settlement Project
The Discovery Programme

(see Farrell, R.T., Kelly, E.P. & Gowan, M. 1989. The Crannog Archaeological Project, Republic of Ireland: A pre-preliminary report. IJNA 18.2, 123-136 and Kelly, E.P. Observations on Irish Lake-Dwellings. In Karkov, C. & Farrell, R.T. (eds.)

Granard

Granard, what are you?
even though small
you are steeped in history
and remembered by both friend and foe
you used to be a rebellious town
but now so civilised.

As a gloom town
you are lived in now
by one who is distraught
by the disappearance of our kin
but you will survive
and live to see another day.

Thomas Donnelly

First published in "Beneath The Moat", Granard Writers' Group 1990

The Flax and Linen Industry in Granard Barony

During the 18th century flax was an important cash crop for the vast majority of small holders in County Longford. Flax grew better on shallow, moory land. The crop was harvested for linen production, one hundred days after planting. If allowed to grow any longer it would produce a poorer quality linen.

In 1698 a law was passed discouraging the manufacture of wool in Ireland and encouraging the manufacture of linen. Robert Stephenson, a Reporter for the Right Honourable Trustees of the Linen Manufacturers for the years 1760-61, considered Longford to be the best flax producing county in Ireland.

Flax growing was highly labour intensive. Production of the crop during the summer and weaving the yarn during the winter kept the people occupied all year round.

Many farmers had a pit for turning the flax and there were bleach yards in almost every townland, including one in Bunlahy. Every house had its weaving loft, where the men wove the yarn which had been spun into hanks or spangles by the women on their spinning wheels (in the kitchen).

In 1796, the Trustees of the Linen Manufacturers published a list of persons to whom premiums for sowing flax had been adjudged. In the Barony of Granard, Patrick Donohoe and James Hart each owned a loom, as they had five acres of land producing flax. There were also 736 spinning wheels in the Barony, each wheel owner had sown at least a rood of flax.

Flax and linen production in County Longford increased steadily from 1700 and reached a peak from 1760 to 1780. The golden era lasted until 1815.

The minutes of the Trustees of the Linen and Hempen Manufacturers of Ireland Tour 1810, report that the markets of Longford and Granard 'are very respectable and extensive'. 'There was an increasing prosperity in the entire community which lead to more marriages and an increase in population'.

Food for the increasing population meant that more land had to be given over to the cultivation of potatoes. A different variety of potato, the Lumper, became popular because of its prolific yield and poorer families had sufficient potatoes to supply three meals per day.

In 1835 there was a severe deterioration in the economic situation in Ireland. A slump had commenced after the Napoleonic wars. The importation of cheap cotton from America undermined the production of linen here. In 1840 linen production was almost forgotten in County Longford, Ireland's most densely populated county. The standard of living in Ireland became so bad, a Commission was appointed to enquire into "the conditions of the poorer classes in Ireland. As a result a Poor Law was passed in 1838 and the building of the Workhouses commenced, including in 1842 a workhouse for the Granard Union.

A report from Granard Union Workhouse, dated 24th April 1845, stated that "oats, rye, potatoes and flax were planted daily" in the grounds of the Workhouse. "Heavy rain retarded the planting."

Flax was grown extensively in the townland of Kilbride on land beside 'Reillys of the stream.' Here the remains of a flax kiln occur. Kilns were necessary where open air drying alone was insufficient to dry flax and fibres for retting. The remains of a stone shed at Mastersons in Cooldoney was known as the "flax shed". Land at Ballyboy, now owned by Mary and Vincent Quinn, was used as a bleaching green. Farmers still living in 2002 can recall seeing wild flax growing near Newgrove before that area was planted by the Forestry Dept. in the 1959-60 era.

The growing of flax and the processing of the plant into linen once contributed greatly to the local economy. This profitable indigenous industry has long since disappeared and linen has become an expensive, luxury cloth.

Sources: Egan, Paddy, The History of Flax and Linen in Co. Longford 1698-1998.In association with Longford Historical Society. Turners Printing Co. Ltd. Longford 1998. Recollections contributed by several local people. Compiled by B.Grier.

THE WEAVER

Tradition dictated that either a red or a green ribbon was tied around the distaff to keep threds in place – red indicating that the weaver was married and green that she was single.

Glossary of terms used in the Flax and Linen Industry

Beetling: Pounding linen to produce a softer texture.
Beit: Sheaf of flax.
Bleaching: Spreading out the flax in the sun to make it white.
Fiddle: Machine for sowing flax-seed.
Gaitins: Putting cured flax in stocks to dry out in the weather.
Green (yard): Place where flax is bleached.
Hackle: Iron-toothed instrument for teasing out flax or hemp.
Hack & Perm: The spinning wheel was changed from wool spinning to linen spinning by changing the "hack" and the "perm".
Memorialist: Representative of linen board.
Retting: Steeping the flax under water to separate the fibres.
Rippling: Removing the seed from the flax plant by flashing across a wooden pole.
Scutching: Beating the flax against a firm object to remove the outer shell of the plant.
Stook: Six sheaves of flax standing in stooks together to dry.
Warp: Threads running lengthways in the loom.
Weft: Threads running sideways in the loom.
Yarn: A continuous strand of spun fibres used for weaving, as distinct from thread used for sewing.

MILITARY BAND — August 1943.

Granard Union Workhouse

(see also pages 20-22 and 112)

The Workhouse for Granard Union was built in the town land of Grassyard, at the junction where Barrack Street meets the roads leading to the more distance parts of the Union, in Counties Cavan and Westmeath. Land originally attached to the Workhouse consisted of 3 acres 2roods 30 perch, increased in 1845 by 7 acres 2 rood 10perch. Cnoc Mhuire, Secretary School is now built on this site.

The plan of the Workhouse building was similar in design to the plans used throughout the country for the accommodation of six hundred persons. The front building at the entrance was in advance of the main building. On the top floor was the Boardroom and clerk's office; underneath were the waiting hall and a room for the Porter. The main structure was a transverse building two storeys high. Wards for males and females were on either side. At the rear, were kitchens, a washhouse and storerooms. A hall /chapel /dining room connected the main building with the 'idiot' ward and the infirmary.

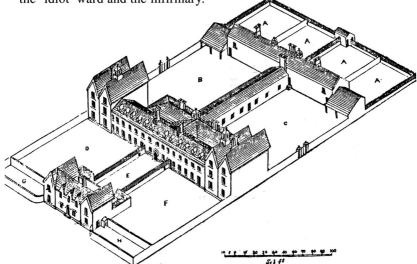

Bird's-eye view of a Union Workhouse. *Illus.: The Irish Penny Journal, 27/02/1841.*

The Workhouse was opened on 30th September 1842. Paupers seeking admission had to prove their eligibility. A ticket signed by three ratepayers and a Parish Warden was needed for entry. The name, age, religion and place of origin of the pauper were recorded in the Workhouse Registers. In return the pauper was given a number, food, shelter, clothing and a straw bed. The able bodied were expected to work from rising time to bedtime. The men broke stones and the women worked in the washroom and also did the "carding". Initially the system worked as had been intended. Things changed utterly from 9th September 1845 when the potato blight was first recorded in Ireland and, as it had no official name, it was referred to as "the potato murrain" or "an dubh".

In the Granard area, in pre-famine days, the Lumper variety of potato was grown in "lazy-beds", the soil worked on with the "loy". This variety of potato was prolific in yield but particularly sensitive to blight which at that time could not be controlled. On the 23rd September the *Longford Journal* reported that "potatoes are selling at 2d a stone" and "there never was such a breadth of them planted in this county". Blight spread rapidly due to favourable weather conditions and so the principal food source was much reduced and the "potato people" would soon be faced with the stark choice, starvation or seek entry to the Workhouse where for many, starvation was a slow process.

As the blight continued the potato harvest diminished, cottiers and out of work farm labourers also sought admission to the workhouse. Ratepayers of rented land, less than a quarter acre in size, had to give up their claim to the land as a precondition for admission. The tide of "human misery" was soon "clogging up every inch of available space". Disease in these overcrowded conditions added to the catastrophe.

In 1845 the number in the Workhouse was 259. On the last week in November 1846 that number had risen to 525 and Granard was classified as "distressed". Sheds for storing straw were used to accommodate the inmates and the Poor Law Union Guardians were given "power to hire additional houses". Springlawn House, Ballinlough House and the Barracks were considered too small as they could only accommodate 30 to 40 "infirm old women". In their efforts to accommodate the ever-increasing number seeking admission The Guardians of the Workhouse considered many options. Galleries were to be constructed in the existing wards, shelters were built at the outer walls and even the construction of additional proper buildings was also considered. While the Guardians debated which option to follow, the blight continued its devastation. On the 30th May 1846 the Clergy and Gentry of Granard held a meeting. S.W. Blackhall Esq; D. L. Coolamber Manor, was in the Chair. He requested funds for the relief of the poor and £181 was subscribed.

On the 11th June, Mr Blackhall, acknowledged The Commission's recommendation of £170 from Lord Heytesbury, Lord Lieutenant and applied for 10 tons of Indian Meal. On the 15th August 1846 a Granard Correspondent wrote in the *Longford Journal* that the future of "the potato crop is such as to furnish grounds for fearful anticipation". These fears were realised. In January 1847 the numbers in the Workhouse increased to 691, of whom 438 were children.

To help alleviate the dreadful conditions Soup Kitchens were organised, initially by the Society of Friends (Quakers) and later by Government agencies. On 6th February 1847 a further subscription of £239 was collected locally. On the 27th February, The Rector Rev. John Shea, wrote from The Vicarage,

Extract from the Longford Journal — 6/2/1847

GRANARD

We feel great pleasure in inserting the following list of subscriptions for the relief of the poor in Granard and the surrounding district:

Richard Greville, Esq.,	(second subscription,)		...	£100
R. G. Davis, Esq.,	do.	do.	...	5
W. Webb, Esq.,	do.	do.	...	3
James G. Murphy, Esq.,	do.	do.	...	5
Nathaniel Callwell, Esq.,	do.	do.	...	5
John Thompson, Esq.,	do.	do.	...	5
Major S. W. Blackall,	do.	do.	...	5
Rev. Mr. Tomlinson,	do.	do.	...	5
Very Rev. Mr. Sheridan, P.P.,		do.	...	10
Rev. Mr. O'Reilly, C.C.,	do.	do.	...	2
Francis Tuite, Esq.,	do.	do.	...	2
The Duke of Buckingham,	...	...	...	20
Rev. Mr. Gregg,	...	...	...	7
A. Lefroy, Esq., M.P.	...	...	...	5
H. Grattan, Esq., M.P.,	...	...	...	3
Mrs. bushe,	...	...	...	2
A. W. Bell, Esq.,	...	...	...	2
Irish Relief Association,	...	...	...	10
Mr. Thomas Pettit, merchant, Granard,	...		...	10

in Abbeylara, to the Central Relief Committee, in Dublin Castle, requesting funds as there were now "747 inmates in the Workhouse". He also suggested, "that a portion of the grant made by the Government might be forwarded to us". The grant in question was for £71. In another letter on 25th March 1847 he mentioned "a ton of rice valued at £24 granted by the Society of Friends for the relief afforded by our soup kitchens to the poor. They are in a famished state and yet perfectly quiet and submissive to the law". On the 1st May 1847 the Fever Hospital was opened in the grounds of the workhouse beside Cartronwillan Lane and this provided further accommodation for 40 persons. A mortuary was also built near by.

It was at this time that "a large body" of men came in to the town from the Lough Gowna Road declaring "that they would never accept soup or, stirrabout but that they were willing to work." Their tattered garments, shaggy hair and grisly beards, gave them a frightful appearance. The Magistrate at the Petty Sessions promised to "endeavour" to have them on the Relief Works on Saturday 1st May. On 8th May 1847 it was reported in the *Longford Journal*, "that a horse had died in the area and had been taken away and used for human food." Conditions for the poor in the Granard Electoral Division continued to deteriorate. Details of soup rations given from the 26th April 1847 show that the highest number receiving soup on any one day was 2701.There were 1,046 on the list when the rations were discontinued on the 29th August 1947. On the 6th October 1847, Rev. William Dawson, C.C., Granard died from fever, "caught in the discharge of his duties" and is buried in Granardkill Cemetery.

On 19th November 1847 the Guardians of the Granard Union were empowered to administer Relief out of the Workhouse for a period of two months. The Guardians had a most difficult time, "facing rising costs and the difficulty of collecting rates". A report in the *Times* of 26/6/47 stated, "Granard Board of Guardians requests, unsuccessfully, its own dissolution due to the intolerable burden of relieving the destitute from local rates". In December 1847 the Union finances were chaotic. Major Blackhall was deputy Vice-Chairman. "His necessary attendance in Parliament deprived the Union of his services and matters in his absence became confused". Only £2,756 was collected in Rates, while debts were in the region of £2,094. The Major personally gave the sum of £100 to meet "current expenditure".

On the 19th February 1848 Mr Flanagan, Inspector, dissolved the Board of Guardians. Vice-guardians (paid officials) were appointed. They anticipated "considerable difficulty with the entangled affairs of the Union". On the 6th April, the Workhouse doctor, Gleadowe Grier L.R.C.L.I., feared disease as there were "930 individuals hourly thronging around the house in increasing swarms". The burial ground at the "back gate" was not properly kept so the Guardians discussed buying some land about one mile distant to use as a Burial Ground.

Nationally the famine was officially declared "over" in 1848. It is difficult to reconcile that statement with the reality of the conditions in

Admission Building of Granard Workhouse. *Photo: Raymond Casey.*

Granard Union Workhouse, where so many were still in residential care or getting outdoor relief. This was also the year when the Guardians sent "twenty four females" from the Workhouse to Australia.

The Workhouse continued to play its part in helping to relieve the poor of the Union. On 3rd November 1855 part of the Administrative Block caught fire and Records such as Minute Books etc. were "consumed in the fire or destroyed by water". Luckily there were no lives lost in the fire; the loss of these books curtails the retelling of the tragic story of life in the Workhouse for staff and inmates. The trauma of that tragic time caused a silence that suppressed talk or discussion among survivors. The fate of the suffering people needs to be told. "A muted dead demand their debt of memory".

The buildings were demolished in the 20th Century. All that remains of the Workhouse now is a section of the boundary wall and the foundation stone marked 1842.

Sources: *Parliamentary Papers. Famine Services (Irish University Press 1970). The Irish Penny Journal 27/2/41 – Vol. 2 pp231-33; Vol. 3 pp389-99; Vol. 4 p.414; Vol. 8 p.325.*
National Archives Relief Commission Papers. RLFC 3/1/3125; RLFC 2/2/16638.
Longford Journal 23/9/45; 30/5/46; 6/6/46; 6/2/47; 27/2/47; 24/4/47; 1/5/47; 8/5/47; 29/5/47; 4/3/48.

Researched by Bernadette Grier.

Granard Union Workhouse Records
December 1844 to April 1845

Week Ending	Inhabitants	Sick	Fever	Died
30 Nov 1844	371	17	2	1
07 Dec 1844	372	17	2	1
14 Dec 1844	375	20	7	0
21 Dec 1844	394	12	9	1
28 Dec 1844	395	17	9	3
04 Jan 1845	419	33	4	1
11 Jan 1845	425	28	4	0
18 Jan 1845	423	61	4	0
25 Jan 1845	431	68	4	0
01 Feb 1845	433	34	1	2
08 Feb 1845	443	33	2	2
15 Feb 1845	446	22	1	1
22 Feb 1845	449	19	1	1
01 Mar 1845	462	20	0	0
08 Mar 1845	455	21	1	3
15 Mar 1845	443	18	3	2
22 Mar 1845	429	31	4	0
29 Mar 1845	440	35	6	1
05 Apr 1845	444	22	2	1
12 Apr 1845	434	40	4	0
19 Apr 1845	433	34	3	0
26 Apr 1845	429	32	5	0
03 May 1845	416	34	5	0

Granard Union Workhouse Records
December 1845 to April 1846

Week Ending	Inhabitants	Sick	Fever	Died
29 Nov 1845	352	22	0	1
06 Dec 1845	361	28	5	3
13 Dec 1845	388	25	5	0
20 Dec 1845	415	26	6	2
27 Dec 1845	418	29	19	0
03 Jan 1846	526	34	19	1
10 Jan 1846	441	31	18	0
17 Jan 1846	452	30	16	0
24 Jan 1846	461	26	16	0
31 Jan 1846	476	24	16	1
07 Feb 1846	474	27	16	2
14 Feb 1846	462	26	11	3
21 Feb 1846	466	26	15	0
28 Feb 1846	466	30	20	2
07 Mar 1846	473	28	24	1
14 Mar 1846	471	29	58	2
21 Mar 1846	472	29	48	1
28 Mar 1846	474	25	43	2
04 Apr 1846	489	23	31	1
11 Apr 1846	489	20	30	2
18 Apr 1846	486	22	19	2
25 Apr 1846	496	24	6	0
02 May 1846	484	21	19	0

Extract taken from the Longford Leader Centenary Magazine.

Famine folklore
Kate Flood. b. 1882, Cranally, Granard, Co. Longford

I heard me aunt say it was nothing to see a woman with six or seven children come into a house that time looking for a bite to ate, and the woman of the house would give her a noggin of milk and stirabout of oaten male. She'd feed the childer first then herself and then on to the next house.

Auld Mrs. Corcoran, the wife of Peter Corcoran, went into Granard Workhouse and took out three children out of it. These three children were belonging to Ballinuty and their father and mother died of the faver, and the childer were brought away to Granard Workhouse.

Inside the green wall of the Workhouse in Granard, where the houses are now, a row of beds inside the wall, and some thatch or something covering them, and all the people in them beds had the faver. And Mrs. Corcoran, she went into Granard with a neighbour to the workhouse and it was believed that if you threw green fruit into each bed, you'd escape the faver. She went and she had the neighbour with her and she had a bag of green apples, and she went along the row of beds, one bed to other and she looking for the childer, and she threw a green apple into each bed she passed, to keep her from bringing home the disase with her.

She got the childer and brought them home with her, the three of them. She had no child of her own. But after a while some friends (relatives) of the childer came and took them away from her and sent them to the United States to friends out there. And I often seen that auld woman crying and she telling that story and how the childer were taken from her and sent to America, after she taking them from Granard Workhouse.

Source: Póirtéir Cathal: Famine Echoes (Gill & Macmillan) Dublin 1995.

St. Patrick's Church, Granard

The Tenison Groves religious census of 1766 shows that 150 Protestant families lived in the Parish of Granard. An 1834 census shows a population of 575 Protestants and 7,223 Roman Catholics.

Records of Births Deaths and Marriages from Parish records from 1820:

	Births	Deaths	Marriages
In the 16 Years: 1820–1836	435	94	69
In the 46 Years: 1836–1982	758	584	199

Source: History of St. Patrick's Church, Granard (R.W. Stafford).

1798 - Battle of Granard

The bi-centenary of the Rising of 1798 was commemorated nationally. Granard remembered those who fought on Wednesday, 5th September, 1798. The map shows the route taken by Humbert from Killcummin Bay to Ballinamuck where the final pitched battle fought in Ireland took place.

Diversions by the United Irishmen were to be carried out at Granard because of its military strategic importance.

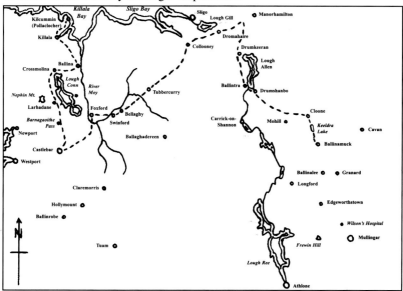

Route taken by Humbert through Connacht – also centres of activity in 1798.

The photo shows the original "Tuites Row 1798" title recently uncovered by P. Harton in 2002.
Photo: Bríd White.

1998 — GRANARD REMEMBERS 1798

Granard people at the 1798 Memorial Cross, beside the Croppy Graves at the church. Many are descendants of the heroes of Granard's struggles. Some are eminent historians. Front row (L–R): Yvonne Keegan, Nora Keegan and baby Eoin, Dorene Farrelly, Niall Keegan, Barry Keegan, John Keegan, David Keegan, Harry Farrelly (with a musket found near Granard and believed to be one of the French guns). Middle row (from the Cross): Susie Forster (nee Denniston), Laura Connell, Mary Connell (with bayonet). Back row: Kevin Connell, Dick (O'Keefe) Monahan, Pat Connell, Tommy Connell, Jimmy Donoghue, Edward (Denniston) Forster, Fr. Francis Kelly P.P., Mattie Connell, Seán Flaherty, Syl Kiernan, Oliver Farrelly.

CORTNAWILLAN LANE – Commemoration Plaque. *Photo: Bríd White.*

Further reference:
Leitrim and Longford, 1798. By Des Guckian. *"Undaunted by Gilbert and Yeos".* Chapter 5, pp15–21.

(see also pages 15, 16, 107, 109, 110, 111)

THE LONGFORD CANISTER KICKERS

The 1908 Old Granard Shamrocks who represented the county in the Leinster Football Championship — Front row: frank Coyle, James (Buck) Creegan, Peter McGovern, Willie C. Kavanagh, John (Parnell) Carters, John Boylan, Paddy Cadden, John Creegan, Bill Kiernan, Martin (Butcher) Bergin, Philip Cadden, Thomas (Tumbler) Boylan, Frank Hynes, Thomas Cadden, James (Pongo) Toby. Back row: James Carr, Thomas Dale, James (Sonny) Kiernan, J. Gavaghan, Joseph Fagan, James O'Hara, Thomas (Aeroplane) Dunleavy, Thomas Monaghan. *Photo: Frank McMahon.*

LONGFORD HARRIERS

Main Street, Granard, 1943 — Father McCormack, L.D. Kiernan, Bernard Masterson, Patrick Flynn, James Carrigy and General Sean McEoin. *Photo: Seamus Carrigy.*

Conor Gearty

Conor Gearty was born at Ballinacross, Granard in 1957. His education began at Granard Primary School, continuing at Abbeylara Primary School, Castleknock College, Dublin and UCD where he studied Law. During this time Conor won the Observer Mace, a prodigious award for debating – open to Britain and Ireland, also the Irish Times Debating Competition.

In his career so far, Conor has been a Fellow of Emmanuel College, Cambridge, Professor of Human Rights Law at King's College, London and is now Director of the Human Rights Centre at the London School of Economics (part of the University of London). He is also a barrister, in practice at Matrix Chambers, Gray's Inn, London.

Conor has written for many newspapers and periodicals on issues of freedom, justice and human rights. He also broadcasts regularly on BBC World Service on these subjects. His books include *Freedom under Thatcher* (co-author) and *Terror*, a political and historical analysis of terrorism.

Noel Monahan

Born in Granard in 1948, Noel Monahan received his early education at Granard Primary School, continuing at St. Norbert's College, Kilnacrott, St. Patrick's Training College, Dublin and completing his Higher Diploma at Cnoc Mhuire, Granard. He is now Deputy Principal at St. Clare's College, Ballyjamesduff, Co. Cavan. A talented poet, dramatist and musician, Noel has published three poetry collections – *Opposite Walls* (1991), *Snowfire* (1995) and *Curse of the Birds* (2000). His poems have been translated into Italian, Romanian and French.

In 2001, Noel won the Poetry Ireland / Sea Cat National Poetry Award and the PJ O'Connor RTE Radio 1 Drama Award for his play: *Broken Cups*. Noel Monahan's work has appeared in many Irish and international newspapers and journals including *The Irish Times, The Sunday Tribune, Poetry Australia, Poetry Scotland* and *Paterson Literary Review*, USA. He has also written and directed musicals which have been performed at local and national level. In May 2002, Noel received an ASTI Achievement Award for his outstanding contribution to Irish literature.

> "The moat wraps its earthy chill of history about us; the Norman invasion, an age of feudal lords and barons, the rage of '98 and past generations trapped in their own space. Up here, we feel our own limitations and all these years these trees and lakes and hills waited for us. We entrust the moat with our deepest feelings and dreams. Almost without knowing it, the moat is dreaming the town and its endurance ... The moat has its secrets ..."
>
> **Noel Monahan**

Sheridan Clan

The Sheridan Clan had its origins in Granard. In early Christian times they were granted the title of "Erenagh" of Granard. This hereditary position as lay lords of the church gave them a high ranking in society. Over the succeeding centuries the Sheridan Clan spread throughout the county of Longford into Cavan. Eventually the Sheridan name was mainly established in Australia, Argentina and the United States of America.

Some famous Sheridan names from the past are Denis Sheridan, born early 17th century, who assisted Bishop Bedell to translate the Bible into Irish; Richard Brinsley Sheridan (1751-1816) a dramatist, orator and a prominent member of the English parliament from 1780-181; General Philip Henry Sheridan (1831-1888) a successful commander of the U.S Army in the American Civil War and Martin J. Sheridan (1881-1918), a renowned athlete, won five gold Olympic medals – four for discus and one for shot put. One of the most famous Granard born Sheridans was Brother Oliver, of the Franciscan Friars of the Atonement, Graymoor, Garrison, New York. He was an outstanding humanitarian and personality who was internationally known for his work among the poor.

In order to reunite those of the Sheridan name and to celebrate their common heritage, an inaugural meeting to organize a Clan Gathering was held in Granard in 1995. The first Gathering was held in August 1966 with Sheridans attending from various parts of Ireland, the United Kingdom, Australia, Argentina, and the USA. The highlight of the weekend was the re-enactment of the Battle of Granard depicting the burning of the original town at Granardkill in the early 14th century.

Clan Gatherings are held biannually when illustrious present day Sheridans are honoured. The young Longford soprano, Michele Sheridan, now internationally acclaimed in the operatic world, has performed at Clan Gatherings. At each Gathering a new Chieftain is elected and it is hoped that the Gatherings will continue as long as the Sheridan name endures.

Plants of Granard area

by Sean Howard
(continued from page 82)

Populus tremula (Aspen) common in many places throughout the area.
Populus alba (White Poplar) quite common in Derrycassan wood also a large mature tree by the roadside at Killasonna.
Betula pendula (Silver Birch) rare in forests and bog margins.
Betula pubescens (Common Birch) very common in boggy ground.
Corylus avellana (Hazel) not very frequent in the area.
Castanea sativa (Spanish Chestnut) obviously planted in Derrycassan wood but it appars to have naturalised in many areas.
Quercus robur (Oak) not very frequent but some good specimens present in the area.
Fagus sylvatica (Beech) very common, some fine specimen trees.
Polygonum hydropiper, common on lake shores.
Sagina nodosa (Knotted Pearlwort) common in the fields between Derrycassan wood and Dring car park.
Tellima grandiflora, this is an extremely rare plant to be found naturalised in Ireland, it grows abundantly in hedges around Creevy and Cloughernal. It most likely spread from a garden in the area.
Clematis vitalba (Old Man's Beard) occasional in forests and hedges.
Ranunculus hederaceus (Ivy Leaved Crowfoot) common in muddy places near Lough Gowna shore.
Erophila verna (Whitlow Grass) occasional on waste ground.
Rubus idaeus (Wild Raspberry) very frequent in forest clearings and hedges throughout the area.
Linum catharticum (Purging Flax) in rocky places on Lough Gowna shore, common.
Hypericum androsaemium (Tutsan) common throughout the area.
Hypericum pulchrum, common on banks in Derrycassan wood.
Lythrum salicaria (Purple Loosestrife) common on parts of Lough Gowna shore.
Epilobium angustifolium (Rosebay) abundant and quite spectacular in cleared or newly planted forest areas.
Epilobium brunnescens, a garden escape native to New Zealand and rare throughout Ireland. It has been found in a disused sandpit in Dring.
Rhododentron ponticum, also a garden escape – it has frequently naturalised in forests.
Lysimacia vulgaris (Yellow Loosestrife) frequent on the lake shore near Derrycassan.
Anagalis arvensis (Scarlet Pimpernell) occasional on paths and waste ground.
Samolus valerandi (Brookweed) occasional on the lakeshore at Lough Gowna.
Ulmus procera (English Elm) Cartronwillan Lane, survivors of Dutch Elm Disease.

Trades and Businesses in Granard - late 1800's - 1980's

Present Owner Occupier	Previous Owner Occupier	Previous Trade(s) Service	Dates

Barrack Street / Main Street (L.S/R.S.)

Present Owner Occupier	Previous Owner Occupier	Previous Trade(s) Service	Dates
J. & H. Kiernan (Springlawn)	Presentation Srs. (Pettits) Mercy Srs. Misses D & R Petit	National School/Workhouse Guest House	1870's 1881-1894 1920's -1958
Macken Family	Macken Family	Filling Station	1967 onwards
P. & M. Brady	Hugh McCabe Tommy McCabe	Tailoring Carpentry	1930's-1980's 1930's-early 1940's
Brady's Garage (Autoparts)	Thomas/Eliz. Cowan Frank McGann Tom, Brian Brady Michael/Frank Brady	Hide, Skin Merchants Solicitor's Office Bicycle/motor repairs Ford/Fiat Dealers Motor repairs, Fiat Dealers	Early 1900's Early 1920's Mid 1920's-1978 1978-1990
Liam Moore	Christy & Janie O'Shea	Tailoring: Secondhand Clothes, Sweet Shop	1920's-1930's T.D.
Emmet Cunningham	Ned Hayden Tim McGahern JJ Cunningham	Motor Repairs/ Agent Shamrock Petrol Motor Repairs/ Agent Shamrock Petrol Welding & Machinery repairs	1920's-1930's 1930's-1949 1959 onwards
Kane's (Flats) Kane's (Garage)	Peter Matthews Patsy & Jackie Lynch Danny Ledwith	Coach Builder Motor Repairs Motor Repairs	Early 1900's 1962-1977 1977-1987
Community Centre/ Resource Centre	W & F Humphry	Sawmill; Electrical Generating (brought Electricity to town in 1926	1920's-1932
	Alpha Cinema (McEvoy, McDonald) Donal Glennon	Picture House Furniture Factory	1945-1966 1970's-1985
Donnelly's Bus Service (Yard)	Jack Devine Overnight Bus Depot: C.I.E.	Bakery/Grocery	1920's - mid '30s 1940's-1967
Tommy Stokes	Mrs Devine Terry Devine	Sweet/Cigarette Shop Bakery	1920's-late 1950's late 1800's-1986
Duggan Family	Simon Reilly Johnny/Jack Collumb	Shoe Maker Grocery/Egg & Fowl Merchant	1920's-'30's 1930's-1982

Present Owner Occupier	Previous Owner Occupier	Previous Trade(s) Service	Dates
Gormans	Paddy Doherty (Silver St.)	Blacksmith	Early 1900's-1950's
Steakhouse (T. Pettit)	Margaret Daly Devoys Joe Simon Reilly Enda Gearty Michael McCarthy	Fish, Fruit Merchant Fruit Merchant Shoemaker Solicitor Electrical goods/grocery/petrol	1920's 1930's 1940's-1950 1953-1954 1954-1990
Thomas Pettit	Tom Drum	Barber	1930-late 1950's
Syl & Marion Kiernan	Thomas Kiernan	Licensed Promises Sweet Shop Auctioneer	1912-early '20's 1920-1930's mid 1800's-1920's
Ann Macken	Bernard W Macken	Forge, Farrier Wheelwrights, Butcher, Cornmill Cafe, B & B	1800's 1900-1922 1936-1960's
J & T Curran	Mr & Mrs Smith	Boarding & Eating House	1930's-1950's
Andy Smyth	Andy Smith (Senior)	Cooper, (Tubs, Ferkins, Churns, Noggins, Beer Barrells)	1876-1962
Kanes	James (Tasty) Burns	Boarding & Eating House	1890's-1960's
Marg. Brady	Grehans	Boarding & Eating House	1890's-1960's
Bridie Rogers	Jim Kellett	Saddler (Saddles, Bridles, Britchens, Collars)	1921-T.D.
	B & H Rogers	General Drapers	1967-1979
Devines (Tailors)	James W. Burns Michael Devine	Grocery Shop Tailoring	1912, 1927 T.D. 1944-onwards
Bank Of Ireland	Hibernian Bank Offices, Residence	Banking Institute	1880 onwards T.D.
M & G Hourican	Parochial House M & G Hourican	Residence of local Catholic Clergy Licensed Premises/Restaurant	1868-1971 1972 onwards
John O'Donoghue	Joe Kennedy Michael Devine	Butcher's Shop Tailoring	Late 1920's 1933-1944
John O'Donoghue	Owen Daly Christopher Daly	Tailoring	Early 1900's -1982 (T.D.)

Present Owner Occupier	Previous Owner Occupier	Previous Trade(s) Service	Dates
Supersams (Chinese Restaurant)	Michael Keegan	Licensed Premises Grocery Shop	Late 1880's-1992
Hartons G.A.A.G. (FÁS) Office Adult Literacy Office	Hugh Brady M C Brady Alan McDonald P M Farrell Noel O Connor	Licensed Premises Grocery & Provisions Funeral Undertaker Newsagents Solicitor's Office Solicitor's Office Mens Drapery	1912 '27, '31 T.D. Early 1930's 1950's 1977 onwards
Libby's Restaurant (Hartons)	Camerons Con Kellett	Drapery Saddler	1912, '14, '27 T.D. 1931 T.D.
Stephen King	McLoughlins Grogans J ORourke	Licensed Premises/Grocery Licensed Premises/Grocery Licensed Premises/Grocery	1927-T.D. 1930's-1970's 1972-1977
Keegans	Biddy Rogers Peter Sheridan Keegans	Sweet Shop Drapery Wool Store	Early 1900's Early 1900's 1930's-1950's
K & B Keegan	Tobins James Keegan	Butcher's Shop Butcher's Shop	Late 1800's 1909 onwards
J Pettit	J J Pettits	Grocery, Hackney, Licensed Premises/Garage, Farm Machinery/Seeds Fishing Tackle	1708 onwards
Paul & Carmel Fay	Larry Ward Tom Smyth/Michael	Licensed Premises/ Grocery Licensed Premises/Grocery	1912, '27, '31 T.D. Early 1940's-1982
McBriens (Harper's Lodge)	Patrick Cosgrove John Walsh Benny Walsh	Licensed Premises/Hardware Licensed Premises/Hardware/ Newsagent, Farm Seeds, Fancy goods, Furniture	1912,'14,'27 T.D. 1926-1995
McBriens	J J O'Reilly John Cullen/Terry Cullen May McIntyre	Drapery, Agent for Educ. Co. Drapery Flats/Sweet Shop	1912-1937 Late 1930's/40's 1960-1968
Bay Horse O'Hara Family	Dolan Family Jos. Tierney Paddy & Pauline O'Hara	Drapery Outfitter, Hosier, Draper Licensed Premises	Late 19th Century 1914-1960's 1970's onwards

Present Owner Occupier	Previous Owner Occupier	Previous Trade(s) Service	Dates
Bay Horse O'Hara Family	John Nugent	Licensed Premises/Grocery Grocery	1912/14 TD
	Pat O'Hara (Senior)	Licensed Premises/Grocery	1914 onwards
	Paddy & Pauline O'Hara	Licensed Premises/Grocery	
O'Haras	Donnelly Family	Pioneer Bus Service	1927 onwards
		Boarding House	1940's-1960's
Mackens (Boomerang)	John Joe Ledwith	Licensed Premises Grocery	1912/'14/'27 T.D.
	S & Harry Devine	Licensed Premises/Grocery	1947-1980
Mackens	J Geraghty	Butcher's Shop	1912-1927
	Tom Connolly/Tom Murray	Butcher's Shop	1927-1935
	Jimmy Macken	Butcher's Shop	1935 onwards
A & J O'Hara	Farrell Kelly	General Drapery	1912/'14 T.D.
	J & D O'Hara	General Drapery	1947-1980's
Ann Walshe	Michael Drumm	Millinery & Drapery	Early 1900's
	Terry & Paddy Leonard (Landlord O'Halloran)	Millinery, Drapery, Boot Retailer	1912/1914/1927 T.D. 1950's
	Stephen, Nan Walshe	Butcher's Shop	1963 onwards
Masterson Fruit & Vegetable Shop	James/Elizabeth Devine	Tailoring, Dressmaking	Early 1900's
	Social Welfare Dept.	Local Office	1960's
Lovett Family (Copper Pot)	John Donohoe	Licensed Premises	Early 1900's-1927
	John Coyle	Licensed Premises	1927-1930's
	Peter Fagan	Licensed Premises	1930's-1960's
Paul Flood	John & Bob Burns	General Merchant	1912/'14/'27/'79 T.D.
	Jack Flood	Auctioneer/Ins. Broker Irish Permanent Agent	1979 onwards
Paul Flood (Looking Glass Hair Salon)	Kate Markey	Shoe Shop, Haberdashery Tobacconist, (Homemade cigarettes from tobacco plants grown in Carrigys)	1920's-1930's
	K Kiernan	School items	1930's
	Alan McDonald	Solicitors Office	Late 1930's-1985
L & B Cunningham	EPM Reilly	Licensed Premises Grocery/Bakery	1912/'14/'27 T.D.
	John McCabe	Coach Builder	1930's-1940's
	Dr. McEvoy	Surgery	
	Dr. C O'Reilly	Surgery	1950's

Present Owner Occupier	Previous Owner Occupier	Previous Trade(s) Service	Dates
L & B Cunningham (Cont'd)	Con Clarke Larry Cunningham M & T McBrien	Petrol Station Supermarket Supermarket	1950's 1960-1980 1980
J V Donohoe	Thomas Markey Edward Kelly John Donohoe	Bakery/Licensed Premises Grocery/Licensed Premises Grocery/Licensed Premises Tourist & Steamship Agent Lourdes Pilgrimages Agent	1800's 1925-1927 1927 onwards
Tom Curran	Patrick Curran K & H Rock	Grocery Grocery/Hairdressing	1920-1945 1950's-1963
Social Welfare Dept.	James Mulligan	St. Mary's Hotel Bus Operator, Hackney Religious Goods Shop Home Grown Fruit General Grocery	1920's-1950's 1950's-1968 T.D.
Rena Kennedy	Egans M & J Drum Agnes Drum/Dan Cosgrove	Publicans General Grocery/Hardware Souvenir Shop Electrical, Bicycle Shop, Musical Instruments	Early 1900's 1908 1928-1960
Kathleen Walsh	Mattie Dolan George Walsh Tommy Walsh	Grocery Shop Grocery, Hackney Hackney	1920's 1932-1945 1945-1952
Padraic McNamara	Beatty's John Rock	Fowl & Egg Merchant Fowl & Egg Merchant	Late 1800's-1900 1920's-1940's
McNamara Family	Frank Kiernan Johnny Moore	Grocery Post Office	Late 1920's-'40's Early 1940's onwards
Gerry Kiernan	Michael Kiernan Brian Masterson L.D.F. Dr. O'Reilly	Draper, Tallow Chandler Butcher's Shop Depot Surgery	1920's-1940 1940's-1949 1949-1960 Early-late 1960's
Mike's Bar (Murray's)	Tom Doherty J Hughes J Finnegan M & M Murray	Tea, Wine, Spirit Merchant Confectionery, Grocery, Coffee Shop Licensed Premises Licensed Premises Licensed Premises	1912/'14'/'27 to '71 1972-1975 1975-1977 1977 onwards
Paddy & Mary Durkin	A & P Cusack Hugh Durkin	General Draper/Outfitter General Draper/Outfitter	1912/1914 T.D. 1924 onwards

Present Owner Occupier	Previous Owner Occupier	Previous Trade(s) Service	Dates
R Finnan	Paddy & Terry Leonard	Boot warehouse	1912-1949
	T Finnan	Drapery	1949-1950's
	J Finnan	Sweet Shop	1980's
Bert Doran	J & E McGovern	Confectioner	1912
		Licensed Premises (Star Bar)	
	James Keenan	Licensed Premises (Star Bar)	1930's
	Mrs Houlihan	Licensed Premises (Star Bar)	1940's
	Victor & Toplis (Houlihan)	Bicycle Shop	1950's-early 1960's
	Tommy Lynch	Licensed Premises (Star Bar)	1964-1975
McBriens Supermarket	Anthony, Felix, John & Massy Slevin	Licensed Premises Grocery/Agent Farm Machinery	1912/'14/'27/'31 T.D.
	Matt Ward	Licensed Premises/Grocery	1920's-1976
	Peter Boyle	Licensed Premises	1976-1979
	J Manning	Licensed Premises/Grocery	1979-1984
MCBriens (Londis)	Peter Flood	Baker, Licensed Premises	1912-1914
	Peter Donoghue	Butcher's Shop	1936-1940's
	Andy Smyth	Butcher's Shop	1940's
	Powers	Bookmakers	1950's
	Brendan Fagan	Cobbler	1960's
John & Kitty Farrell	J & Rose Montfort	Frapery Shop (Mainly corsets) Dressmaking	1912-1927
	Tuthills	Fancy Goods	Early 1950's
	RM Manus, B Reynolds	Fancy Goods	1954-1972
M Sheridans	Mrs J Ward	General Drapery	1912-1914 T.D.
	M Sheridan & Paddy Reilly	General Drapery	1932 onwards
Brid White	Mary Jane Kiernan	Leather Stores Showmaker	1912-14,1927 T.D.
	Annie Cosgrove	Shoe Shop	1930's-1960's
		Temporary accommodation for CC	1970's
	Ann Gormley	Antique Shop	1984-1987
	McEvoys Med Hall	Pharmaceutical Chemist	1987 onwards
McKeons	James/Larry Cosgrove	Fancy Goods	Early 1900's-1982
	K & D Looker	Fancy Goods	1982 onwards
Jimmy Finnegan	Peter/Larry Kiernan	Hardware & Grocery Shop, Undertaking	1886-1920
	J Finnegan	Ladies, Gents Drapery	1949 onwards
Market House	Urban Council	**Ground Flood - Market area**	1691 (old building)
		Longford Co. Branch Library	Mid 1950's onwards
		Town Clerk's Office	1938-1978

Present Owner Occupier	Previous Owner Occupier	Previous Trade(s) Service	Dates
		Upper Floor - District Court	(Monthly) 1924 on
		Venue for Harp Balls	1791-1785
		Recreational Activities	
		Temporary Technical School	1948-1953
Paul & Chris Flood	William Mullen	Greville Arms Hotel	1891-1903
	LD Kiernan	Greville Arms Hotel	1903-1966
	Misses McCarthy & O Neill	Greville Arms Hotel	1966-1979
	Paul Donohoe	Greville Arms Hotel	1979-1983
Pat Sheridan	Kiernans Stores	General Hardware	1909-1952
		Licensed Premises	
		Funeral Undertakers	
		Builders Providers	
		Grocery, Hardware	
	Gallons	Hardware	1952-1956
	Heatons	Drapery	1956-1972
	Brian Brady	Store	1974-1977
	Pettits & King	Wholesale/Retail/Furniture	1977-198
Maguire Family	Imperial Hotel	Bakery/Licensed Premises	1890's-1930's
	(Phillips)	Accommodation/Hardware	
		Original Bus Stop	
	Mr Francis	Dentist's Surgery	1930's
	Margaret Cosgrove	Flats & Hairdressing	1940's-1960's
		Church Organist	1930's-1960's
J McEvoy	Joe Tierney	Drapery	1920's
	McEvoys	Medical hall	1923-1987
P & C Fay	Paddy O Donnell	Licensed Premises	1930-1960
	P & G King	Licensed Premises	1960-1988
P & B Masterson	Flanagans	Bakery, Landowners	Early 1900's
	Peter Heslin	Bakery, Grocery	1920-1960
	Mick Heslin	Licensed Premises	
	S & C Hourican	Electrical, Bicycle Shop	1961 onwards
		Licensed Premises	1961-'82
G & R Garland (Smyths)	Eugene Drumm	Grocery, Wine & Spirits Glass, China, Delph Warehouse	1912/1927
	Stephen King (Sen)	Drapery/Licensed Premises	1930's
	Stephen King	Furniture Store	1950's-1975
Donoghue's	Burns & Co (The Lady)	Grocery, Animal Feed	1912-1930's
	Jimmy Cunningham	Grocery, Animal Feed	1930's-1972
	J & S Donoghue	General Hardware	1972 onwards

Present Owner Occupier	Previous Owner Occupier	Previous Trade(s) Service	Dates
Donoghue's	W T Moody	Watchmaker	1912, '14, '27 T.D.
	Miss Early	Homemade icecream & sweets	1940's-late 1950's
J. Donoghue	E Grier	Pharmaceutical Chemist	1912/'14/1931 T.D.
	B Macken	Grocery, Electrical applicances	1940's-1990
Phil Smyth	M Kelly	Licensed Premises/Grocery Timber Merchant	1912/'14/'27 T.D.
	Delia McCann	Licensed Premises	1921-1951
	Smyth Bros	Licensed Premises	1951 onwards
McWades	Thomas Markey	Royal Hotel	1912 T.D.
	Tommy Reilly	Royal/Eagle Hotel	Early 1920's
	Sybil McGann	GP	1927-1954
	Frank McGann	Solicitor	1927-1949
	V & E Tierney	Hairdressing/Hackney	Early 1960's
	Dick King	Solicitor	1954
	Enda Gearty	Solicitor	Mid 1950's-1969
	McWades	Hairdressing	1970's
Mrs. Morrissey	Dominic & John Irwin	Post office, Grocery Leather Stores/Stationery	1912/'14/'27/'31 T.D.
	Martin McCawley	Grocery/Hardware	Early 1930's-'46
	J Morrissey	Grocery/Hardware Agri Machinery, Animal Feed	1946-1990
	John Brady	Egg & Fowl Merchant	
Choices	E P Irwin	Pharmaceutical Chemist	1912, '14, '27, '31 T.D.
	JT Leahy	Pharmaceutical Chemist	1932-Late 1970's
Garda Siochana	Royal Irish Constabulary	Military Barracks (Barrack Sq. in Denniston Park area)	Early 1900's-1922
	Garda Siochana Barracks	Offices & Residence	1922 onwards
		New Building	1976
Ned Molloy (SuperValu)	McGahern's Garage	Motor Repairs, main Austin Dealers	1954-1960's
	Longford Arms Motor Works	Motor Repairs main Austin Dealers	1960's-mid '60's
	G Dinan	Motor Repairs, Farm Machinery	1965-1971
	K Devine	Bakery Van Repairs	1971-1979
Credit Union	Biddy Curneen	Grocery Shop	1920's-1950's
H. & D. Farrelly	Ellen Reillly	Grocery Shop	1920's-1930's
T.P. & M. Smith	John/Paddy McNally	Blacksmith	1920-1940's
M. McCarthy	John Mahon	Cooper	1920's

Present Owner Occupier	Previous Owner Occupier	Previous Trade(s) Service	Dates
	Hamills	General Store (sold crubeens) Travelling Shop	1930's
	Killeens	Labour Exchange	1935-1946
	Pat & M McCarthy	Labour Exchange Confectionery Shop	1946 onwards
Tyre Centre (M McDonagh)	Jim Kellett Cathy/Dick Kelly	Harness maker Sweet Shop	1915 Late 1950's-'80's
Mastersons	John Killala	Tin Smith	1920's
O & K Cassidy (G.A.P.)	Yorkes Dr. Yorke Pettit J Lee	Boarding House Doctor's Surgery Gents Hairdresser	1920's 1920's-1940's 1963-1979
Sacred Heart Primary	William Thompson Hayden Family	Landowner/Emigration Agent Licensed Premises Bakery/Mill/Grocery	Early 1900's 1920-1963
	Sisters of Mercy	Temporary Secondary School Classrooms	1968-1971
Convent of Mercy	St Josephs Industry	Knitwear (machine & hand)	1961-1987
Cnoc Mhuire Secondary School	Guardians of Union Workhouse	Workhouse	1842-1932

Market Street

Mary & Ann OReilly	Kitty McIvor	Licensed Premises Bookshop	1919
	K McCluskey/O'Reilly	Licensed Premises	1929-1960
	Rita O'Reilly	Licensed Premises (Central Bar)	1960's onwards
F & B McMahon	Johnny Moore	Post Office	Late 1930's
	Vincent Tierney	Shoe Shop/Hairdressing	1950's
	Kitty O'Connell	Dressmaking Registry Office (Thompsons)	1919-1950's Early 1900's
	Mary McCabe	Restaurant	1931 T.D.
	Paddy Murray	Sweet/Fruit Shop	
	Mr Francis	Dentist	Late 1930's
F Campbells	Thomas Kiernan (Scottie)	Hucksters Shop	1930's-1940's
	John Campbell	Butcher/Draper	1950's onwards

Present Owner Occupier	Previous Owner Occupier	Previous Trade(s) Service	Dates
Mrs M Murtagh	Paddy McCluskey	Grocery Shop	1940's
S & N Carr	Jim Conlon	Egg Merchant	1927
	Jimmy Flynn	Blacksmith	1930's
	H Rock	Egg & Fowl Merchant	1942
	Jack Carr	Grocery	1969 onwards
Crane Yard	Urban Council	Rented Garage Spaces Pluck House, Blacksmith's Forge Venue for FunFairs & Carnivals	1940's
	John Scanlon	Motor Repairs	1978-1990's
Des Cummins	E Kane	Licensed Premises & Grocer	1912, '14 T.D.
	Pat Kinlan	Licensed Premises & Grocer	1927-1943
	Simon Cummins	Builders Providers	1943-onwards
Pat the Bakers	CornMarket	Sale of Grain	Oldest building in town
	Donnellys Bus Service	Depot & Repair Garage	1940's-1970's
Derelict Houses	M Mahon	Sweet Shop	1920's-1930's
	M Early	Egg/Fowl Merchant	1931
	F Dolan	Bicycle Shop	1950's
Ken Looker	Luke Reilly	Grocery	1950's-1970's
Ulster Bank	Offices/Residence	Banking Institution	1869 onwards
Bank Lane	Mickey Coyle	Cobbler	1940's-1950's
Buttermarket	Urban Council	Sale of Market produce	1893
Garvey's	Phil & Tommy Cadden	Painter, Decorator Sign Writer	1931-Late 1950's
Mrs. Coyle	Padna McNally	Blacksmith	1930's-1950's
J Mulligan	Willie Strong	Carter (goods from Ballywillian Station)	1930's
	Johnny Maguire	Bicycle Shop (Repairs in Buttermarket)	1940's-1950's
J Breslin	P. & R. Sheridan	Bakery, Restaurant Grocery & Provisions	1924-1984
E O'Hara	Patrick O'Connor	Grocery	1920's
	M Sheridan/Majore	Grocery	1930's
	National TV	Electrical Shop	Mid 1970's-1979
T Pettit	John & Mary Reilly	Grocery	Early 1900's
	Newman Brady	Hackney, Delph, Leather Store	1920-1972

Present Owner Occupier	Previous Owner Occupier	Previous Trade(s) Service	Dates
	Finnegans	Fish & Chip Shop	1972-1974
	P & V Scanlon	Light Hardware	1974-1979
S & N Carr	Ned Murphy	Restaurant, B & B Hackney Service	1900-1931
Carrs	Mr Rice	Barber	1920-1930's
	Larry O'Brien	Grocery	1930's
	Jack Carr	Grocery	1959-1969
Colm Flood	John W Burns	Licensed Premises	Late 1800's-Early 1900
	J O'Connor	Licensed Premises	1931 T.D.
	Benny Hague	Licensed Premises	1940's
	Bill Moore	Licensed Premises	Late 1940's
	Kathleen Boyle	Licensed Premises	1950's-1958
	Dr Murtagh	Licensed Premises & Surgery	1958-1964
	Fintan/Colm Flood	Licensed Premises	1964 onwards

St. Colmcille Terrace / Scrabby Road

P & E Neary	P Tynans	Grocery Shop	1935-1974
No.9 St Colmcille Tce	Jim Small	Grocery Shop	1950's-1980's
Redmond Tce	Con Comiskey	Wheelwright	Early 1900's

Dublin Road/Ballalley

J V Donohoe Yard/Outhouses	Paddy Nedley	Blacksmiths Forge	Early 1900's-1930's
Shed R S Road	H Doherty	Blacksmith's Forge	1930's
Patsy Martin	Ms Devine/McCann	Light Grocery Shop	Late 1930's
Mrs Williams	Mrs B Carr	Basket Making	1920's

St. Patricks Terrace

G Carters	J & F Parkes	Tailoring	1920's-1940's T.D.

Present Owner Occupier	Previous Owner Occupier	Previous Trade(s) Service	Dates

Moxham Street

Present Owner Occupier	Previous Owner Occupier	Previous Trade(s) Service	Dates
Michael Maguire	J McAllister	Metal Worker (ploughparts)	1920's-1930's
Pat the Bakers (Residence & Offices)	Joe Regan	Light Grocery	Late 1940's
	Charlie Doyle	Builder	1920's-1940's
	Mick Mulligan	Bicycle Repair/Hackney	1950's-1980's
	Wesleyan Chapel (1758)	Methodist/Catholic worship	1822-1867
	B Tallon & A Flynn	Motor Repairs	Late 1950's
Rear of Street Buildings	Michael Kelly	Timber Yard	1869-1920's

Longford Road

Present Owner Occupier	Previous Owner Occupier	Previous Trade(s) Service	Dates
Pat the Baker (Offices)	Steegans	Clothing Manufacturer	1974-1982
	Christine Fashions	Clothing Manufacturer	1984-1987
Tully Family	Tully Family	Commercial Body Building	1970 onwards
Ardscoil Phadraig	Longford VEC	Vocational School	1953 onwards

Abbeylara Road

Present Owner Occupier	Previous Owner Occupier	Previous Trade(s) Service	Dates
Mrs Peggie O'Reilly	Conal J. O'Reilly & Son	Auctioneer & Valuer	1902-2002
Des Cummins	Thomas Kiernan Thomas Quinn	Granarda Ballroom	1955-1981
(Adjoining vacant site)	Granard Co-op Dairy Society Ltd	Creamery & Stores	1903-1927
	Longford Co. Co.	Cattle Loading Bank	1950's-1967
	John McCabe	SawMill	1947-1949
	Pat McCabe	SawMill	1949-1954

Carra Road

Present Owner Occupier	Previous Owner Occupier	Previous Trade(s) Service	Dates
Dr N. Donohoe	Dr T J Donohoe	Surgery	Late 1960's onwards
Brian Gormley	Brian Gormley	Vetinerary Services	Early 1960's onwards

Barrack Lane

Present Owner Occupier	Previous Owner Occupier	Previous Trade(s) Service	Dates
Eircom	Telecom Eireann	Telephone Exchange	1970's onwards
Old Site	FCA	District Head Quarters	1960 onwards
Old Site	Government Offices	Local Office	1970's-1980's

Compiled by Sister Maeve Brady, Granard, from folk memory of town residents (especially Maureen McCarthy, Tommy Kelly, Nan Macken, late John Macken — also Thom's, MacDonalds, Connaught & Leinster Trade Directories.

1920 — $25 BOND CERTIFICATE

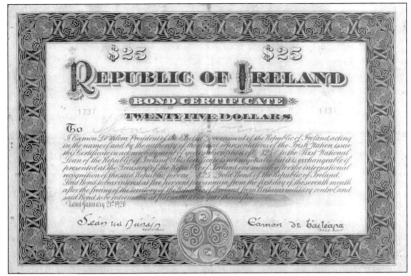

Bond bought in New York by Thomas Wrenn, Aughnagarron.   *T. Grier.*

GRANARD CREDIT UNION

New premises opened 23rd May 1999.   *Photo: Joy Burns.*

Granard in the new Millennium

The town continues to thrive, although the population has dropped to around 1000, as shown on the recent census. Local businesses and enterprises are flourishing and 'Pat the Baker' is a household name nationwide. Convoys of commercial vehicles arrive and depart day and night from local industries. Garages do a brisk business supplying farm vehicles throughout the country. Donnelly's Buses continue to provide transport far and wide. The farmers' marts on Mondays and Wednesdays generate extra business in the town. Every Friday morning, home produce, made by members of Country Markets Ltd., is available at the Market House.

Education in Granard caters for all age groups. The Granard Community Playgroup has relocated to the Old Boys' School on 'The Hill'. The two Primary Schools are amalgamated in the Sacred Heart School. Cnoc Mhuire and Ardscoil Phadraig provide a high standard of education for second level students. Other new educational facilities include Granard Area Project; the Adult Learning Centre, Youthreach and Outreach.

The Sports Complex at Higginstown caters for a variety of recreational activities: G.A.A., pitch and putt and tennis. The Complex is also the venue for the annual Agricultural Show. Granard continues as a centre for Equestrian events.

The Rath Mhuire Resource Centre is an inspirational haven for body and soul. A varied programme of cultural, creative and educational activities is provided. The Community Centre is home to set dancers, drama, whist drives, a flourishing Harp School and various parish events.

A highlight of the year 2002 was the rejuvenation of the streetscape of Granard. A dramatic painting programme was undertaken using co-ordinated heritage colours. This project was sponsored by Longford Co. Council and by Longford Community Resource Ltd. The visual impact of this unified community effort, is a celebration of colour and a source of delight to all.

The office at Main Street of Granard Area Action Group and FÁS has become the central hub of the town welcoming locals and tourists alike.

Sources

Allen, F.H.A.; Whelan, Kevin; Stout, Matthew: Atlas of the Irish Rural Landscape, C.U.P. Irl 1997.

Boylan, Edward J.: The Parish of Mullahoran.

Bun-Fhleadh: Granard Harp Festival Bi-Centenary 1781-1981 Granard Festival Committee, 1981.

Bun-Fhleadh 1982 & 1983: Granard Harp Festival Granard Festival Committee, 1982 & 1983.

Curtis, Edmund: A History of Ireland. London: Methuen, 1936.

D'Arcy, Gordon: The Guide to the Birds of Ireland. Dublin: Dollard, 1891.

Egan, Paddy: The History of Flax and Linen in Co. Longford 1698-1998. Turner's Printing Co., 1998.

Gaffney, Kathleen; McCarthy, Olive and Yorke, Concepta — Index to forts of County Longford: AnCO/Longford Historical Society Research Project, 1983.

Guckian, Des: Leitrim & Longford 1798. Turner's Printing Co., 1998.

Harbison, Peter: Guide to the national monuments in the Republic of Ireland: Gill & Macmillan, 1975.

Hayes, Richard: The Last Invasion of Ireland.

In Great Haste: The letters of Michael Collins and Kitty Kiernan edited by Leon O'Broin: Dublin: Gill & Macmillan 1983.

Irish University Press Series of British Parliamentary Papers. Copies or extracts of correspondence relating to the state of the Union Workhouses in Ireland. First, second and third series.

Kennedy, P.G. and others: The Birds of Ireland – an account of the distribution migrations and habits as observed in Ireland by P.G. Kennedy, Robert F. Ruttledge, C.F. Scroppe assisted by G.R. Humphreys. London: Oliver & Boyd, 1954.

Kennedy, Patrick G.: Notes on primary education Granard and vicinity 1800 to 1870 – Granard: Patrick G. Kennedy, 1980.

Kerr, Donal: The Catholic Church and the Famine, Columba Press, 1996.

Kinealy, Christine: This Great Calamity. The Irish Famine 1845-50, Gill & Macmillan 1994.

Lane, Padraig: Ireland – London: B.T. Batsford, 1974.

Lewis, Samuel: A Topographical Dictionary of Ireland: London: Lewis, 1837.

Litton, Helen: The Irish Famine – an Illustrated History, Wolfhound Press, 1994.

Longford Journal.

Longford Leader: A Century of Longford Life: 1897–1997.

MacGearailt, Gearoid: Celts and Normans – Dublin: Gill and Macmillan 1969.
MacGivney, Rev. Joseph: Placenames of the County Longford – Dublin: Duffy, 1908.
MacNamee, James J.: History of the Diocese of Ardagh – Dublin: Browne & Nolan – Dublin.
Macken, B.: Folklore and notes (unpublished).
The Midlands: Longford-Cavan-Laois-Westmeath-Roscommon-Monaghan-Offaly/edited by Leo Daly, Dublin: Alberting Kennedy, 1979.
Mimnagh, John & Seamus: To the Four Winds – Famine Times in Ireland, Westmeath Examiner, 1997.
Monahan, John: Records relating to the Diocese of Ardagh and Clonmacnoise – Dublin: M.H. Gill & Son, 1886.
Montague, John: The Dead Kingdom – Mountrath: Dolmen Press, 1984.
Moynihan, P.M.: An Appreciation of Michael Collins.
Ní Bradaigh, Cáit: Granard Folklore (unpublished).
Ó Cathaoir, Brendan: Famine Diary, Unabridged from The Irish Times Series, Irish Academic Press, Dublin – Portland OR.
Ó Siadhail, Michael: The Gossamer Wall – Poems in Witness to the Holocaust. Bloodaxe Books, 2002.
O'Connor, John: The Workhouses of Ireland. The Fate of Ireland's Poor, Anvil Books, Dublin 1995.
Ordnance Survey of the County of Longford, field name books, 1836-1837 – No. 11 – Parish of Granard, Barony of Granard.
Póirtéir, Cathal: Famine Echoes, Gill & Macmillan, Dublin 1995.
Praeger, Robert Lloyd: The Botanist in Ireland – Dublin: Hodges Figgis, 1974.
Prendergast, John P.: The Cromwellian Settlement in Ireland. Dublin: Mellifont Press, 1922.
Taylor, George and Skinner, Andrew: Maps of the roads of Ireland – Shannon, Irish University Press, 1969.
Teathbha: Journal of the Longford Historical Society (Secretary: Jude Flynn).
The Irish Penny Journal No. 35, Saturday 27 Feb 1841, VOL. 1.
Urban Archaeology Survey: County Longford, Part IV, Contributions by A. Halpin and Heather A. King.
The Journal of Ardagh & Clonmacnoise Antiquarian Society, Vol. I & II.
Vocational School, Granard: Project on Granard Folklore.
Warrilow, Stephen: Granard's Standing Stones: L.C.R.L., 1997. Rapid Print Ltd., Longford.
Weir, Anthony: Early Ireland: a field guide – Belfast: Blackstaff Press, 1980.
Woodham-Smith, Cecil: The Great Hunger: Ireland 1845-1849. London: Hamish & Hamilton, 1962.
Woods, Cedric S.: Freshwater Life in Ireland. Dublin: Irish Academic Press, 1974.

Index

A
Annals	p 143
Archaeological Sites	p 146,147
Ardagh	p 10
Aungier, Sir Francis	p 10,12
Annaly	p 08,10,12
Abbeylara	p 09,10,20,50,88
Aughamore	p 05
Annals, Four Masters	p 05,07,38
Act of Union	p 13,16
Abbey St. Mary's	p 33,50,51

B
Bruce, Edward	p 09,50
Baronies of Granard	p 10,11,13,139
Battles of Granard	p 05,07,159,160
Black Pig's Dyke	p 05,33,37
Ballinlough	p 15,18,20,24,78,80
Ball Alley	p 16,30,86
Bully's Acre	p 22
Ballymacrolly	p 23,91
Barracks Military	p 12,26
Bunlahy	p 27,66,94,99,120
Butter Market	p 28,52,53
Ballywillan	p 81,87,88
Borough	p 13,14
Bailey	p 129,140
Bronze Pin	p 137
Businesses	p 165,176

C
Crannog	p 05,148,149
Conmaicine	p 07,08
Cartron	p 10
Charter James	p 12,13
Castlenugent House	p 14,18
Cartonwillan Lane	p 12,31,52,53,55
Cromwell	p 12,13
Cottingham, Major	p 15,16
Collins, Michael	p 23,71,143
Clonfin Ambush	p 24,25
Convent of Mercy	p 32
Cloughernal	p 36,48,133
Cartronbore	p 36,37,133
Carraig na h-Uaine (The Rocks)	p 37,52,53
Cornmarket	p 52,53,97

D
Derragh Lake	p 05
De Lacy, Hugh	p 08,
De Tuite, Richard	p 08,09,129,137

De Lacy, Walter	p 09
De Grenville, Geoffrey	p 09
Dungan, John	p 69,74
Denniston, Alex & Hans	p 15,16,109,110
Druids Altar (Dolmen/Cromlech)	p 37

E
Edgeworth, R.L. & W.	p 139

F
Finea	p 12
Farrell, Patrick	p 05,15
Fair Green	p 28
Flax	p 19,150,151
Famine	p 22,112,151,152
Fairs	p 94,95,96,97
Fort, Baker's	p 38
Fort, Ring	p 05,38,140,141

G
Grotto, Lourdes	p 47,52,53
Granardkill	p 05,09,12,22,129,130,134,135
Gusacht, Bishop	p 07
Gilchrist, Patrick	p 16
Granard, Earl of	p 16
Greville, Fulk	p 16
Greville, Richard	p 22,39,69
Greville Arms Hotel	p 23,24,52,53,68,71,122
Gowna Lough	p 37,51,78,79
Granardkill Church	p 42
Granard Walk	p 52,53
Granard Poem	p 110,111

H
Humbert	p 15
Harp Festival	p 14,26,124
Hempenstall	p 16
Hunt, Granard	p 99,100

K
Killasonna	p 10,18,66
Kinale Lough	p 05,33,34,35,37,78,79,148
Kiernan, Kitty	p 23,71,72,81,143
Kelleher, D.I Philip	p 23
Kinale, Book Shrine	p 05,34,135
King, James	p 10,12
King, John	p 09
King, Henry VI	p 10
Longford, Lord & Lady	p 14
Littleton, G. Fulk	p 16
Land League	p 23

L
Linen	p 150,151,152

M
Motte (Moat)	p 02,15,16,27,33,35,43,52,53,100,105,130, 140,143,145
Market Street	p 17,22,86,97,98
Market House	p 24,52,53,54,97,98
Mc Eoin, Sean	p 24
Methodist Church	p 46,47,52,53
Masonic Hall	p 16,48,49
Mills Lane	p 52,53,55, 65

N
Norman Occupation	p 08,09
Nugent	p 10,19
Names, Family	p 76

O
O'Carolan	p 14,26
O'Donovan, J.	p 138,139
O'Farrell	p 08,09,10,12,13,51
O'Connell, Daniel	p 19
O'Brien, Bronterre James	p 55,69
O'Reilly, Brendan	p 74

P
Plunkett, W	p 10,11
Penal Laws	p 13,14
Parnell, C,S	p 23
Parnell Row	p 31,86,104
Presbyterian Church Tully	p 47
Pin	p 137
Place names – local	p 85
Piseogs	p 118

Q
Quakers	p 154

R
Rivers	p 78,80
Rathcronan	p 12,38,100

S
Sheridan	p 163

T
Teffia	p 05,07,08
Táin	p 07
Tuite's Lane (Row)	p 15,17,30,52,53
Town Commissioners	p 27
Town Hall	p 32,62,97,119,120
Trades	p 165-176

W
Workhouse	p 151,153
Warrilow	p 133,146,147

Acknowledgements

Bank of Ireland, Granard
Sister Maeve Brady
Misses Yvonne, Alison and Linda Burns
British Museum & British Library
Mr. S. Carrigy
Mr. A. Corcoran
Rev. Owen Devaney
Mrs. A. Donohoe
Mrs. J. Donoghue
Mr. S. Donnelly
Mr. & Mrs. M. Flynn, Ballymacroly
Folklore Commission
Mrs. Susan Forster (nee Denniston)
Mr. G. Garland
Mr. E. C. Gearty
The Late Rev. Canon F. Gilfillan
Miss A. Gillooly
Mr. S. Howard
Mr. D. Kennedy
Mr. T. Kiernan
Miss Marion Kearney
Co. Librarian Longford/Westmeath
Mr. P. Masterson
Mr. R. Monahan
Mr. T. Monahan
Mr. H. McGahern
National Library of Ireland
National Museum of Ireland
Office of Public Works, Chancery Lane
Mrs. Mary O'Reilly, Granard Branch Library
Misses Pettit
Sisters of Mercy, Granard
Mr. J. Slevin
Mr. Phil Smyth
Mr. R.W. Stafford
Trinity College, Library
Mr. Ian White

2002 ACKNOWLEDGEMENTS

Martin Morris, Archivist
Mary Reynolds, Co. Librarian
Ann and C. Brady
Christina Kirwan Grier
Oliver Cassidy
Rosemary Gaynor, Granard Library
Bríd White
Very Rev. Canon F. Kelly, P.P.
Credit Union Granard
Keith Millar
Longford Community Resources Ltd
Seamus Carrigy
Nan Macken
Margot Gearty